1.95

S0-DQX-182

Basic Beliefs

in Genesis and Exodus

GOD'S WORD TODAY II

A New Study Guide to the Bible

Emil A. Wcela

Basic Beliefs
in Genesis and Exodus

PUEBLO PUBLISHING COMPANY

NEW YORK

Nihil Obstat: John P. Meier, S.S.D.
        Censor Librorum

Imprimatur: ✠ James P. Mahoney, D.D.
        Vicar General,
        Archdiocese of New York

Design: Frank Kacmarcik, D.F.A.

CONTENTS

PREFACE

Interest in the Scriptures continues to grow. Men and women individually and in groups read, reflect on, discuss, pray from the Bible. I have taught, led, participated in such groups. This participation has convinced me that, despite all the worthwhile material on the Bible already available, there are still gaps to be filled for those people who truly care about the Bible but have had little or no preparation to extract its riches.

Several excellent guides to the Bible exist in the format of booklet series in which each volume provides commentary and explanation on a separate book of the Bible. However, for someone becoming acquainted with the Bible, to work through each book one by one can be a formidable task.

Other books focus on themes and main ideas distilled from the whole Bible. As valuable as such theologies and over-all views are, there is still a need for a familiarity with the *text* of the Bible itself.

In this series, substantial portions of the Scriptures — extensive enough to convey style, language, tone — are the indispensable starting point. Essential background and explanation are provided and the lasting import of the text is suggested. Possibilities for individual or group reflection are offered.

When the reader has completed this series, he will have encountered many themes and main ideas, and this through a selected and guided reading of the text itself. This over-all view can be filled in by further study of the individual books of the Bible.

The general plan emerges from a listing of the titles in this series. It is my strong recommendation that anyone using the series begin with Volume I. If the principles presented there are grasped, the spadework will be done for understanding what follows.

"Indeed, God's word is living and effective, sharper than any two-edged sword. It penetrates and divides soul and spirit, joints and marrow; it judges the reflections and thoughts of the heart" (Hebrews 4:12).

CHAPTER I

BEGINNING

SETTING OUR SIGHTS – WHAT TO EXPECT

Picking up the Bible can be a frightening and discouraging experience.

People have heard of the importance of the Scriptures and many decide to take the plunge. They move in deep earnest – and logically. They open to page 1 and fully intend to keep reading until the cover is closed on the last page.

Genesis fares not badly. The stories are interesting and lively, even if sometimes puzzling. Talking snakes? Floods? The early parts of Exodus with their vivid accounts of the plagues and liberation from Egypt hold attention.

But soon nagging questions cause a kind of restlessness. Some of these questions may be very deep and personal ones about God. What kind of God kills the first son of each family? What kind of God wipes out armies by opening and closing seas?

Other questions may arise from plodding through lists of laws covering slaves, property damage, loans, religious practices, and so on. These spring up in the latter chapters of Exodus and come into full bloom in the books called Leviticus, Numbers and Deuteronomy.

Did God really have to specify in great detail all the dimensions and decorations of the sanctuary that the people would use for worship? Is God really the great vestment designer

1

that he seems to be in regulating the garments for the priest?

We come to grips with these questions, with the Old Testament, and indeed with the Bible as a whole, only if we are willing to accept certain ground rules before beginning our study. These ground rules have been treated in some detail in the first volume of this series. For the sake of convenience, we can summarize them here.

God and his truth have become known gradually — and never completely. This has happened in a unique way, over a period of time through God's influence on the history of the people of Israel, then of the Church, chosen by him to be the instruments of his work among men. It happened in the life and actions of special individuals who spoke for him, acted in his name.

These people, these individuals, remained part of their time. The insights and experiences they had of God they presented in language, in symbol, in expression, very much affected and formed by the thought patterns, the culture, the social conditions, the historical situations through which they lived.

Since the Old Testament was hundreds of years in the making, it reflects different ways of expressing the divine truth. Basic beliefs were passed from generation to generation. They were deepened, enriched, challenged, reinforced, by changes in the world of the people expressing them. Each generation added details, descriptive material, laws, professions of faith, that made the tradition more alive for its own time.

We have to approach our reading of the Old Testament expecting to find all the styles of writing and speaking that people of the time used; poem, creed, proverb, love song, war chant, and the like. We must also expect to find a different idea of history than the one to which we have becomed accustomed. There will be more concern with communicating the *meaning* of an event than with the specific details of the event. In order to communicate this meaning, details are very often added — details that we would call unhistorical because they do not correspond to the blow-by-blow description that we would want. However, for the Israelites, they expressed the significance of the event, *how God was doing something for his people.*

This summary is by way of signpost pointing out some of the factors that will be operating as we work our way through key parts of the books of Genesis and Exodus to focus on certain basic beliefs.

The procedure in the following pages will be this: Certain texts will be indicated, which *must be read, carefully, several times.* Then a brief commentary will attempt to fill in the important background, to clarify meaning, to indicate more emphatically where the issues for faith are.

J, E, P – THOSE MYSTERIOUS LETTERS

Israel told its story its own way, or rather its own ways. Not surprisingly, different groups among the Israelites preserved the sacred traditions. Each of these groups had its own special theological emphases, its own insights, its own style of presenting and teaching these traditions. Eventually these traditions were formed into large-scale works about the beginnings of Israel. These works no longer exist as such. We know of their existence from the traces they leave in the first five Books of the Bible as it is now.

The stories of creation, Abraham, the Exodus from Egypt, etc., are not simple, straightforward, from the same time, the same place. Many of these stories are a combination of three accounts of the same event from different times and places, or of a basic story line revised, elaborated on, seen afresh, by successive generations.

However, we are not told this explicitly. We follow out
the clues to this conclusion. Some of these clues will be
discussed in considering the text. The three original accounts
or noticeable sets of revisions go by the names "J," "E,"
and "P."

J stands for the "Yahwist tradition," "J" being the first
letter in the German spelling for Yahweh. The designation
comes from the fact that a hint leading to the suspicion
that different blocks of traditions had been worked together
was the use of two different Hebrew names for God, Yahweh being one of them. The Yahwist tradition was a more
or less complete story that began with Paradise and the
fall, continued through Abraham and Moses and the plagues,
and ended with the death of Moses. Scholars believe that
J comes from Jerusalem in the tenth century B. C., from
the court of David or Solomon.

E stands for the "Elohist tradition." Elohim is the other
name used for God. E began with Abraham, took in the
events in Egypt, and ended with the death of Moses. This
form of Israel's traditions came from the northern kingdom,
probably in the ninth century B. C.

P signifies the "Priestly tradition." P also contained stories
of creation and the flood, but its main interest was in collections of laws and regulations that have to do with worship, with the Temple and the priesthood. P apparently
represents some of the traditions preserved by priests at
the Temple of Jerusalem. Although put into its final form
sometime around the year 500 B. C. it contains much more
ancient material.

What all this means is that Genesis and Exodus as we now
have them are a complex combination of earlier material.

Imagine three histories of America; one written in 1800 by
a highly patriotic school teacher in Boston, a second written in 1900 by an amateur historian in South Carolina,

and a third, the work of a clergyman with religious inter-
ests living in New York in 1950. Imagine someone in 1970
making these into one without bothering to take out inconsistencies and repetitions, leaving out a good deal from all
three, and adding his own further insights and interpretations.
This suggests some of the complexity of the present form
of the stories of deliverance and creation.

THE HISTORICAL BACKGROUND – WHO WERE THE HEBREWS?

For the Exodus, the time is the thirteenth century, B. C.;
the scene, Egypt. In a number of places (e. g., Exodus 1.16;
1.19; 2.6, etc.), the people associated with Moses in the
story of liberation from Egypt are called "Hebrews." This
term seems to be connected with the name "Apiru," given
to groups of people in documents found in various parts of
the Near East and dating from the 1800's to the 1100's
B. C.

Scholars believe that "Apiru" or "Hebrew" referred originally to a certain economic or legal status rather than to
nationality or race. "Hebrews" had no homeland of their
own. They settled within or near the borders of the developed lands where they might obtain food, water, work. As
stateless foreigners, they had no rights in the lands to which
they attached themselves for longer or shorter periods of
time. Texts from Egypt tell how some of these Apiru were
pressed into service by a number of Pharaohs to build temples and fortresses. Very likely, these are the forced laborers
we meet in the accounts of the slavery and oppression in
the Book of Exodus. Not that the Egyptian documents
and the Bible are necessarily talking about the exact same
group of people, but that the oppressed people in Exodus
fit against a background of social circumstances illustrated
by information from outside the Bible.

The story of a group of such people is a story of liberation
brought about by a liberating God.

SUGGESTIONS FOR REFLECTION

1. What was the series of events or inspirations that brought you to desire to read the Bible?

2. Have you ever personally felt about your life that "God was at work in it doing something for his people"? That there was a *meaning* in it you were unable to understand or fathom at the time?

3. Can you parallel your life experiences with those of the Hebrews in each of the following?

a. The stories of Genesis and Exodus are a combination of three accounts or traditions originating in different circumstances and developing over the course of time. Do your relatives ever give different versions about things that happened in your family in years past? Can you see any ways in which your family traditions have been developing, becoming stronger, or declining over the years?

b. The Hebrews were called out of the slavery of Egypt by the providence of God. Have you ever had the experience of being "called" in some unique way from a bondage or slavery to a liberation?

CHAPTER II

YAHWEH BROUGHT US OUT OF EGYPT

THE CALL OF MOSES AND THE NAME: YAHWEH

Please read: Exodus 3. 1—21

The faith of Israel believed that God intervened in the drudgery and suffering of this oppressed and homeless people wearing away their lives on the building projects of the Egyptians.

The history of God's dealings *with* men is one of dealing *through* men. In the great act of liberation that God would accomplish and that would have repercussions on all succeeding human history, a central figure would be the man, Moses.

Israel would make much of Moses. But there was never any doubt that the real power, the real mover, was God. In the accounts of Moses that Israel transmits, before Moses does anything, he encounters God.

How does one meet God, this God who has no body, no visible form?   The faith of Israel tried to express the experience of meeting God in many ways. Two of them come together in Moses' experience of the burning bush.

First, "an angel of the Lord appeared to him."

Whatever the validity of later developments, the meaning of "angel of the Lord" here has to be gotten from the use of the term in the Old Testament. The main thing "angel" conveys is not the familiar being with long hair and flowing robes. In the earlier parts of the Bible, "angel of the Lord" refers to God himself insofar as he shows himself to men.

One Biblical tradition has it that no man can see God and live. God's presence is so overwhelming that man would be destroyed by contact, much as a moth is consumed by contact with the flame of a candle. And yet God, in his own way and on his own terms, does make his presence felt. One way of expressing this experience of God's presence is to talk about "seeing an angel." The angel is both God and not-God. To "see an angel" is to experience an awareness of God reaching into man's world and at the same time to confess that no man ever sees God in his overpowering wonder.

Generally, when the Bible speaks of man coming into contact with an angel, the experience is one of the God who protects, helps, saves; God who shows great familiarity with men; God who attracts men to himself.

In other words, to say that "the angel appeared to Moses" is to say that Moses had a real experience of God, but one that can never be described in words that convey all that really happened. The important thing was that the people of Israel were convinced that all Moses did was the result of God's touching his life.

Further, the angel appeared "in the fire flaming out of a bush." Fire is another common Old Testament symbol for God. When believers try to express the inexpressible, they reach for a wide stock of signs. Everyone hearing about the fire in which an angel appeared would know that Israel was saying that Moses had met God.

THE CALL OF MOSES

Why did God cross Moses' path?

8

The reason is found in the words attributed to God. "I have witnessed the affliction of my people in Egypt . . . I know well what they are suffering. Therefore I have come down to rescue them from the hands of the Egyptians and lead them out of that land into a good and spacious land, a land flowing with milk and honey . . . Come, now! I will send you to Pharaoh to lead my people, the Israelites, out of Egypt."

But Moses has reservations about this splendid sounding task. "Who am I that I should go to Pharaoh and lead the Israelites out of Egypt? " Again, "When I go to the Israelites and say to them, 'The God of your fathers has sent me to you,' if they ask me, 'What is his name? ' what am I to tell them? "

In chapter 4, there are more objections. "Suppose they will not believe me or listen to me? " "If you please, Lord, I have never been eloquent . . . but I am slow of speech and tongue."

THE NAME "YAHWEH"

The substance of God's response to all this hedging by Moses is "I will be with you . . .I am who am . . .This is what you shall tell the Israelites: I AM sent me to you."

"Thus shall you say to the Israelites: The LORD . . .has sent me to you."

Here we meet in an impressive setting the proper name of God in the Old Testament. In many translations, this name is brought into English as "Lord." This volume, using the New American Bible, follows its practice. Wherever the name "Yahweh," appears in the Hebrew text, the English writes it as "Lord" in capital letters.

The original meaning of the name "Yahweh," is a subject

of much scholarly discussion. However, how the Book of Exodus understands the name is clear in the text. "Yahweh" is taken to come from the verb, "to be." God calls himself, "I am," "He is."

"Am" or "is" are rather pale and colorless words in English. They need something to finish them off. "I am hot." "He is old." "She is a teacher." "I am," or "he is" or "she is" do not make much of a stir by themselves.

But in Hebrew, the forms of the verb "to be" are not just links between a subject and another word describing that subject. "I am" is a strong and pregnant affirmation. The one who makes that statement is proclaiming the strength and power of his existence. To further define "I am" by adding "who am" stresses that the only limit to his existence is the one who is speaking himself.

There is no question of "I am a policeman" or "I am strong" or "I am important." No description fits God properly except God. Only his life and being are rich enough to portray him. All other words and categories are inadequate.

The chief characteristic of this all-present, indescribably powerful reality of God will become clear in the rest of the Old Testament. The name "Yahweh" designates the power of God acting to save his people. Both Israel and Egypt will experience Yahweh, but in different ways. Israel as a power to save, to free; Egypt, as a power to overwhelm and destroy since Egypt stands in God's way.

SUMMING UP

This chapter emphasizes the following insights about God that should challenge our faith and reflection.

God Is Savior. Throughout history, he will show himself as the liberator of the oppressed. The experience of oppression deepens from physical slavery to the more horrifying bondage of what seems like a meaningless and empty life. As this happens, God presents himself as the only savior from even this.

God Acts through Human Instruments. "Instrument" may be an objectionable word since it seems to reduce man to a thing, but it is hard to find another word. The point is that God enters human history through the people who live that history and, indeed, create it. Most of the experiences that are described in extraordinary terms — Moses' conversation with God, for example — are attempts to convey the idea that the persons involved were convinced in faith that God had moved them.

God Gives Himself to His People. The revelation of his name, and the series of objections are meant to indicate that what happens is not the result of Moses working himself up to the conviction that God was speaking to him. Moses' objections show his human inadequacy, that he is not taking the initiative. God's power fills this frail man to demonstrate what God can do. Only God can accomplish man's liberation.

God Controls History. God controls the whole course of human history. Though men are free and act freely, there is a long range plan which is God's and which will not be frustrated. That we do not understand that plan is a problem of our patchwork experience. We must watch the total plan of God work out in slow and separated moments.

SIGNS AND WONDERS – THE PLAGUES

Please read: Exodus 7. 1-11, 10

THE MEANING OF MIRACLES IN THE OLD TESTAMENT

To read through these passages is to be pulled into a rapidly spinning whirl of the unusual. Rivers of blood. Carpets of frogs. Clouds of mosquitoes. Thick darkness. All these, and more, afflict the land of Egypt.

The words characteristically assigned to these events are "signs and wonders." There is a difference between "sign and wonder" and *our* notion of miracle.

For us, "miracle" is commonly understood as some phenomenon of nature which is so far beyond the powers and capacities of natural causes that it can be explained only by the intervention of God.

A man breaks his leg. The leg is set by a doctor and through six or eight weeks heals. The cast is removed and the man is able to walk perfectly well again. This is to the credit of the medical profession and to the normal resilience of the human body.

But consider another case. At 4:50 on Wednesday afternoon, a man's left leg is six inches shorter than the right. This condition has persisted for years. At 4:51 on the same Wednesday, the left leg is exactly the same length as the right. There has been no operation, no medical treatment to account for the change. Something beyond the natural seems to have taken place.

And if there had been some religious activity involved — if, for example, at 4:50 the afflicted man had been lowered into the baths at Lourdes — then at least believers would be sure that God had been at work, that this was a miracle. We could see something that stumped the medical experts, that the "laws of nature" did not cover, and would attribute this to the Supernatural, to God.

The point of view of the believers who molded these parts of the Old Testament was very different. Something was a sign or a wonder not because it was "outside" or "beyond" the laws of nature. Everything — events usual and unusual, the situations of history, the doings of daily life — was under the control of God. There were no "laws of nature" which somehow held together until God bent them out of shape or blew them to smithereens by some explosive exercise of his power. Everything came from and was explainable by God.

What made a sign or wonder was not abnormality but illustrative value. An action or an event was a sign or a wonder because it showed God's invisible power at work.

There was – and is – no way to *prove* God as the cause of something. That God is behind an event or an action is a matter for faith rather than for demonstration with microscope or telescope or whatever scientific tools might have been available 3000 years ago. Something that happens can be interpreted as a sign, or wonder, or miracle only by the one who looks with the eyes of faith. Another might look on the same event and see only a chain of ordinary cause and effect.

Two nomads standing on a sand dune could have watched a group of former forced laborers moving quickly through the desert away from the borders of Egypt. One might have said, "Well, another band of slaves has finally had enough and is trying to make its getaway. Good luck! " The other might have said, led to this insight by God, "Yahweh, the God of Israel, is liberating his people from the oppression of the Egyptians."

All of this has to be kept in mind as we work our way through the plagues and other "miracles" in the Old Testament. A miracle or sign or wonder was more a matter of interpretation by the on-looker or hearer than self-evident fact. But once the Old Testament man of faith was convinced that something was a miracle, i. e., a work from God, a pointer to God, then he was much more interested in relating what happened in such a way as to make it clear to others that God was at work than he was in describing with strict historical accuracy what actually went on.

To put it another way, a modern man or woman and a person from the Old Testament would express experiences they believed to be from God in different ways. I might meet a certain man in whose goodness I would recognize the presence of God. If I were to describe him, I would stick to literal details, how he impressed me with his kindness, his patience, his understanding, and so on. Then I might add, "This man really brings home God's presence."

Another person, looking on exactly the same events and the same person, might have a different interpretation. "This man is psychologically incapable of getting angry or being resentful." What the man conveys depends on the interpretation given, *but* we are careful to *keep the description and the interpretation separate.*

Those who kept alive the stories of the Exodus did not consider this kind of distinction. Once they were convinced that God had acted in the events of the liberation from Egypt, they conveyed their conviction in the way they told the story. They felt free to elaborate on details in order to underline their belief that God was at work. For them, the interpretation of the event was included in the way they told the story of the event.

All of this is not to deny the possibility that the accounts in Exodus and the rest of the Old Testament could be literally true. It in no way contradicts the possibility that God could intervene and change in a spectacular way the ordinary manner in which things happen. It simply proposes that we get ready to read the stories of the plagues and other parts of the Old Testament with the point of view of those who handed them on and wrote them down. Accounts may not be quite so simple and straightforward and literal as they seem.

DIFFERENT TRADITIONS OF THE PLAGUES

Previously, we considered briefly J, E and P, those mysterious letters which stand for collections and revisions of traditions of Israel's early days. These were gathered and preserved at various stages of Israel's history. As separate entities, they no longer exist. However, as threads that have been woven into the story of Israel's beginnings as we now have it, we can pick them out with varying degrees of clarity and certitude in different parts of the Pentateuch.

Taking the first plague of water turning into blood as an example (Exodus 7.14-25), there are a number of inconsistencies that appear to the careful reader.

Take the matter of the wonderful staff. In verse 15, Moses has it. In verse 17, Yahweh seems to have it. In verse 19, Aaron has it. Only a slight suspicion of inconsistency, granted. By itself, the one observation might be passed over.

But within that same story, there is another slightly off-key note. Almost all the references are to *the waters of the Nile river* that are going to be affected by the change of water into blood ("the river" in vv. 17, 18, 20, 21, 24, 25). But standing out in verse 19 is the command to strike *all the waters* throughout Egypt; rivers, canals, marshland, reservoirs, in tubs or jars. If this were at the end of the account of the plague, it could simply represent holding to the last a report of the awesome succcess of the plague. However, immediately after it, the story goes back to talking only about the water of "the river."

Then again, in 9.6, after a plague on the livestock, the text says, "All the livestock of the Egyptians died." But later in verses 20 and 21, there is still Egyptian livestock left alive to be threatened by the plague of hail.

These instances are just that — instances. But as they multiply throughout the plague account, they show that not all fits together smoothly. The most likely explanation is that a final author or editor took over different accounts, J and P at least, put them together and was not at all disconcerted by the wrinkles and rough spots.

15

But it would be rash and unperceptive to dismiss the account as simply a "cut out and paste together" operation, a patchwork which has no overall view. The inconsistencies are there. But the whole is carefully held together by themes that run throughout. These themes spotlight the divinely taught lessons.

The following chart will illustrate how thoughtfully the character of Pharaoh is developed.

What Happens and Pharaoh's Reaction

Genesis 7. 23, water turns into blood, Pharaoh "turned away," "no concern"; Genesis 8. 4, frogs overrun the land, Pharaoh "summoned Moses," "Pray the LORD to remove the frogs," "I will let the people go"; Genesis 8. 24, plague of flies, Pharaoh said "I will let you go to offer sacrifice to the LORD . . . provided that you do not go too far away. . ."; Genesis 9.27f., hail storms, Pharaoh said "I have sinned again! The LORD is just; It is I and my subject who are at fault. . . I will let you go." "But he. . . became obdurate. . . and. . . would not let the Israelites go."; Genesis 10. 8ff, threats of locusts, Pharaoh said "You may go. . ." but not your children; Genesis 10. 24ff., Pharaoh said People may go with children, but may not take flocks.

Pharaoh's character is developed through his reaction to the plagues. He is brought slowly to recognize the awesome power of God working to liberate his people. At the same time, Pharaoh keeps putting himself in the way of God's plan. He fears losing the convenient slave labor that keeps his building projects going. He learns through bitter experience the power of God and the futility of obstructing it.

There is an obvious lesson in the *aim* of the plagues. "I will bring . . .the Israelites out of the land of Egypt so that the *Egyptians* may learn that I am the LORD" (7.4-5). *Pharaoh* will learn the saving power of Yahweh which destroys those whose meddling tries to interfere with him (7.17, 8.6, 8.18, 9.14, 9.29). In 10.2, the *Israelites* will "know that I am the LORD."

What will be known about Yahweh is expressed several times. "So that you may learn that there is none like the LORD, our God" (8.6). "That you may know that I am the LORD in the midst of the earth" (8.19). "That you may know that there is none like me anywhere on earth" (9.14). "To show you my power and to make my name resound throughout the earth! " (9.16). The whole drama between Pharaoh, Moses and Yahweh is played out with the final result that Israel, the Egyptians, Pharaoh, all experience that Yahweh is Yahweh, that he is truly a saving power and presence liberating his people. For Israel, his presence brings good. For the Egyptians and Pharaoh, who stand in human pride against the God of all, his presence is destructive. And this "knowing" of God's power is not an intellectual operation but is experienced through God's action in history.

WHAT HAPPENED DURING THE PLAGUES?

By now, the meaning of the narrative of the Exodus from Egypt should be fairly clear. Israel's faith saw this departure from slavery as a "sign," a "wonder," i. e., a manifestation of the power of Yahweh exerted on behalf of his people. Yahweh showed that he was truly Yahweh by what he did in Egypt. Events that took place some 1250 years before the birth of Jesus, when viewed with the eyes of faith, were and are a demonstration of the life of Yahweh, the God of Israel.

What were those events? What really happened? We cannot be as sure as we might want to be. Why not? Because, as was indicated previously, we are not dealing with a simple and straight-forward eye-witness account. We have at least two different accounts of the plagues, separated from each other by distances in time and place. We have the final version put together hundreds of years after the events. There is theological interpretation worked into the details of the story itself.

To add still another complication, at least for getting strictly historical information, more than an educated guess would conclude that the story of the liberation from Egypt took its shape and was preserved by repetition in the liturgical celebrations of Israel. The story was kept alive and handed on through recital at occasions when the people of Israel came together to celebrate their deliverance from Egypt. Forms of prayer and worship must have had an influence on the way the story of liberation took form.

Taking all this into consideration, there are two main lines of thought about the historical character of the stories of the plagues. One maintains that the plague accounts are fundamentally historical. The events recorded are similar to natural phenomena known in Egypt. The "water into blood" could very well be the reddening of the waters that takes place each year when the Nile floods and becomes discolored by the deposits it sucks up. Frogs are common in Egypt and multiply quickly in intense humidity. And so on for the rest of the plagues.

What makes these natural phenomena signs of the work of God is the extreme seriousness of the plagues (the reddening of the waters does not usually kill fish). Frogs become a frightful affliction rather than just a nuisance when they spread everywhere. Furthermore, that so many disasters occur immediately after one another and that Moses announ-

18

ces the beginning and the end of each also points to God's hand.

The other viewpoint suggests that the narratives of the plagues were so greatly influenced in the process of formation and telling, both as liturgy and literary work, that it is no longer possible to determine exactly what happened.

There is no doubt that some phenomena accompanied the Exodus from Egypt. What these were, how intense they were, how long they lasted, and so forth is just beyond our ability to recover.

IN SUMMARY

We cannot describe exactly all that happened when the Israelites fled from Egypt. But flee they did. Certain phenomena accompanied their flight. Israel's faith professed that both the flight and the accompanying events were the work of God. God was demonstrating that he was their God, that he was a liberating God, that he was God of all the world, even of Egypt and its mighty king. He was involved in a process that would ultimately lead to liberation from that most cruel of human oppressors, Sin.

THE PASSOVER: LITURGY

Please read: Exodus 12. 1-13. 16

In this part of the Exodus story, we are much more obviously dealing with liturgy. Liturgy includes those external actions that the community proposes or accepts as expressions of its inward religious faith and feelings.

Liturgy can involve "re-presentation." The community recognizes some event or action of the past as deeply significant for its present religious life. That past action embodies in a unique way the relations between the people and

19

its God. But liturgy, as re-presentation, is not simply an attempt to keep alive the memory of something that happened in the past. The symbolic ritual makes the past action present now.

Israel lived liturgically. The experience of liberation from Egypt was an experience of the saving power of Yahweh who had chosen and cared about his people. But Egypt was an oppressor, an enemy, an obstacle, of the past. Israel's history was full of new oppressors, new enemies, new obstacles. And Israel's liturgy brought the saving power of God to bear in these new crises.

Israel's liturgy was also a foretaste of the future when there would be a final and definitive saving act by God. One day God would overcome all that stands in the way of his loving will for mankind.

Liturgy for Israel, by the way, was not a manipulation of God. The authentic faith of Israel never believed that God had to hop when the right words were pronounced, the right acts performed. God's power was present in ritual and symbol because he freely willed it that way. And he freely willed it that way only when Israel brought itself totally, in heart and mind, as well as in body, to worship.

The Passover celebration was the liturgical expression of the liberation from Egypt.

THE PASSOVER STORY AS LITURGY

That this is liturgy is suggested by a careful reading of the passage. Much of it is a series of instructions about how the ceremonies are to be carried out, similar to the "rubrics" that can be found in books of liturgy today.

A study of the development of the Passover liturgy provides

much food for thought because there are indications that the ritual is an adaptation of rites practiced by people who did not share the faith of Israel.

The two main parts of the liturgy are:

a. the slaughter of the lamb and the sprinkling of its blood on the door posts of the home (12.1–13; 21-27)

b. the ritual connected with the use of unleavened bread or mazzoth (12.14-20; 13.3-10).

Similar celebrations are known from other cultures around Israel.

The lamb ritual was practiced by flock-keeping nomads just before their springtime move to new pastures. A lamb was slaughtered and its blood sprinkled on the tent posts to drive off evil spirits who might harm the flocks as the females were about to give birth to their young. If the evidence is complete enough to be believed, the Hebrews practiced this ritual even before the time of Moses. However, for one special group of these Hebrews who had been liberated from Egypt, this spring celebration took on a new meaning. Not simply a departure from old pastures and a move to new ones, the Exodus was a definitive departure to the freedom and pastures of the promised land. These Hebrews gave their old ritual new meaning. Now it would commemorate the liberation that God worked on their behalf.

In Canaan, the land in which Israel was to settle, the native farmers celebrated a ritual suited to their way of life. Usually, the housewives of Canaan pulled a handful of leavened dough from what they were going to bake as the day's supply of bread and set it aside. This handful was mixed in with the dough for the next baking and leavened that dough. This process of saving some of the dough of each day to leaven the dough of the next went on all during the year.

However, in the spring, when the barley harvest first came in, the old leaven was thrown out and a new lump begun. For a number of days, since there was no leaven to make the bread rise, flat unleavened bread was eaten. This was done to mark a new beginning. The barley harvested signified a fresh start for the farmers and they commemorated this by throwing out the old and making new leaven.

When Israelites settled in Canaan, they found this spring-time ritual. Since they too were making a new beginning, starting life in a new land, they eventually took over the local ritual and gave it a deeper, more spiritual meaning. For them, it commemorated the new beginning to which they had been led by the power of their God who was settling them in a new land.

Eventually, these two celebrations, found among other peoples but given new meaning to proclaim Yahweh's relationship to Israel, were united into one feast as described in Exodus. The details of celebration as described are the instructions the Israelites developed for the festivities.

The Israelites, familiar with two springtime feasts, gave these new meaning. The killing of the lamb, tied to moving out of old pastures and into new ones, and the unleavened bread, connected with new beginnings of harvest, were reinterpreted by Israel. These rites now made present in symbolic form the moving out of the old slavery in Egypt and the new beginning in the land of Canaan.

Israel's faith believed that all of this was due to God's direction. Hence they had no hesitation in ascribing to God all the ritual instructions for the celebration of the feast. And they believed that in that celebration, they were coming into contact with that same saving presence that had freed them from Egypt and given them all the hope of a new beginning.

SUGGESTIONS FOR REFLECTION

1. "The history of God's dealings *with* men is one of dealing *through* men." Can you recall any time in your life history that this was true?

2. "How does one meet God, this God who has no body, no visible form? The faith of Israel tried to express the experience in many ways." What are the occasions when you *meet* or have ever *met* God? Can you describe them in your own words?

3. If an "angel" or "fire" were both Old Testament symbols of the experience of God, what symbols of God's presence do we acknowledge today?

4. God's power is sometimes thought of as a two-edged sword: a power to save, and a power to overwhelm or destroy. Have you ever been aware of it in this way, i. e., simultaneously saving and destroying what stands in its way?

5. What new insights into the meaning of "angel" have you received from this reading?

6. Spend some time reflecting on each of the following insights into God, especially as they have been experienced in your personal life history of faith:

a. God is savior

b. God acts through human instruments

c. God gives himself to his people

d. God controls history.

7. In the accounts of Exodus and other parts of the Old Testament, was strict literal, historical truth always the most important consideration in the minds of the tellers or writers of the accounts? How can these biblical accounts be squared with our modern notions of historical truth?

8. Pharaoh learned "the power of God and the futility of obstructing it through bitter experience." Have you ever found the same to be true in your life experience?

9. What did the *Egyptians* learn about God from experiencing the plagues? What did the *Israelites* learn about the Lord from this same experience? Did both Egyptians and Israelites learn the same thing in the same way? What role did faith play in this experience? Have you ever shared a common experience with someone else, and then each of you arrived at different interpretations of it because of differences of faith?

10. What does it mean to say that liturgy is a "re-presentation" of a past action now? How did Israel embody liturgically the experience of liberation from an oppressor or enemy? Do we today have such a liturgical re-presentation of the experience of liberation from an enemy?

11. In the history of the Israelites, some pagan practices were adapted and given new meaning to show their relationship to the one God, Yahweh. This was true of the springtime rites to depict the "new life" of faith. Can you think of any secular or cultural practices that Christians have adapted to express spiritual realities of faith? Are there any signs or symbols in your life that have taken on new meaning because of your faith?

CHAPTER III

SING TO THE LORD

THE CRISIS AT THE SEA OF REEDS

Please read: Exodus 13. 17-15. 18

After the hasty departure of the Israelites from Egypt, as Exodus recounts the story, Pharaoh had a change of heart. He and his courtiers complained, "What have we done! Why, we have released Israel from our service! " (14.5).

The fickle Pharaoh, still unconvinced of a divine plan in what had been happening, assembled his army and set out in hot pursuit.

The geographical indications are somewhat confused. Very likely, the Israelites moved to the south and east, to a chain of lakes that are now incorporated into the Suez Canal. There Pharaoh's army caught up with the fleeing Israelites. Accounts of what happened are preserved in this section of the Book of Exodus. The events as described in Exodus have been vividly portrayed in the movie, *The Ten Commandments.* Shimmering walls of water tower above the heads of the Israelites as they pass through the sea, only to collapse and swallow the pursuing Egyptians.

THREE VERSIONS

To understand the Exodus story, we must emphasize again the kind of presentation we are dealing with, one made up of several different accounts of the same event woven into a single narrative.

The earliest account of the events at the Sea of Reeds is the victorious war cry sung by the Israelites in Exodus 15. This is summarized in 15.21:
"Sing to the LORD, for he is gloriously triumphant; horse and chariot he has cast into the sea."

The J account probably took form some two to three centuries after the event, although based on earlier traditions. Scholars identify the J account as the following verses: 13. 17-22; 14.5-7, 10-14, 21b, 24-25, 27b, 28b, 30-31. Excuse the complicated nature of this kind of analysis but it is the only way of working seriously through the account. To simplify, the story that emerges from combining these verses runs something like this.

The Egyptians trap Israel in a camp by the sea. The Egyptians are not able to come closer because of a cloud that separates them from the Israelites. During the night, a wind drives back the water and turns part of the sea bed into dry land. Just before dawn, Yahweh "looks on" the Egyptian camp and throws it into confusion. The Egyptians begin to flee across the dried sea bed. Yahweh then causes the water to return over the Egyptians. At dawn, Israel sees the dead Egyptians on the sea shore.

Notice that there is no mention of walls of water heaped up, no anxious procession between them.

The P account, finalized some 700 years after the event, includes: 14.1-4, 8-9, 15-18, 21-22, 26-27a, 28a, 29.

Two things are characteristic of this account. It is the most "wonderful." Here Israel passes between towering walls of water; here is the tumble and crash of these walls upon the heads of the Egyptians.

The P account is also built up around a theology of the word. God's word brings all things into being, creates and forms history. There is the same emphasis on God's word in the P story of creation in Genesis.

14.1-4: prediction of pursuit
14.8-9: and so it happened

14.15-18: prediction of passage of Israel between the divided waters
14.21-22: and so it happened

14.26: prediction of return of waters on Egyptians
14.27a, 28a: and so it happened.

The story of the passage through the Sea of Reeds is another instance of the special kind of historical writing of the Israelites. This could incorporate varying accounts of the same event in one finished work. This causes problems for our history, but not for the theology of Israel or our own.

THEOLOGICAL INFLUENCES ON THE REED SEA ACCOUNT

Worked into the account of what happened at the Sea of Reeds are two theological ideas from the Old Testament world not exactly familiar to moderns.

The first theological notion is the *Holy War.* Israel believed, with a faith that was just beginning to appreciate the kind of God who had chosen it, that Yahweh was most certainly a God of his helpless and oppressed people. One kind of helplessness and oppression was that experienced in the face of enslaving kings and nations. Certainly the intervention of Yahweh could be expected when his people tried to throw off or defend themselves against this type of oppression.

In the Holy War, Israel believed that the just judge, Yahweh, did more than merely get involved in its battles. Actually, they had only to trust in him and he would do the fighting for them. This is expressed very well in 14.13-14. Moses encourages the frightened people who see the Egyptian army at their heels. "Fear not! Stand your ground, and you will see the victory the LORD will win for you today. These Egyptians whom you see today you will never see again. The LORD himself will fight for you; you have only to keep still."

A second important theological notion is the *Sea as a symbol of Chaos*. The Near East saw the wild and turbulent sea as a fit symbol for the powers of disorder. The god who could bring order and calm to the sea was the god who could bring order and harmony out of all the tossing and confused forces in human history and the universe. In the creation story, God begins creation by "dividing the waters," by bringing earth out of them, by making the waters recede to places determined by him.

Here too, God divides the waters. This is another aspect of the creative power of Yahweh. He is forming a people for himself. The powers opposed to him, the powers of Chaos — represented by the sea and the Egyptians, — stand in the way of his plans. But his power is so wonderful that he uses the sea, the very embodiment of Chaos, to overwhelm the human instruments of Chaos. What greater proof could there be of the tremendous power of God!

The story of the passage through the sea is told incorporating ideas and theological notions of a past time and culture. Perhaps the image of a God who fights wars, who destroys human enemies is repugnant — and it is no longer a part of our Christian tradition. But there is still a valuable truth, that God's saving power will inevitably conquer. Those who erect their own ideas and plans into divinities, those who stand against God, will ultimately find their projects in ashes, their existence empty of true life and meaning. God will triumph despite the worst efforts of man's sinfulness.

WHAT HAPPENED?

The religious lessons of the story of the passage through the Sea of Reeds have been established.

Efforts to determine the exact events that took place end with a minimum that runs something like this.

The liberated Israelites were in danger of annihilation or recapture from a pursuing Egyptian army. God then acted to save his people from this new danger. The Egyptian army was destroyed in a "sea." This was a real event, although the exact details are no longer ascertainable with evidence of the type that historians today might wish. Israel became a new kind of people, learning to trust its God whose might and rule it believed it experienced in these events.

SUGGESTIONS FOR REFLECTION

1. The story of the salvation of the liberated Israelites at the Sea of Reeds has long been used in the Christian liturgy for the Easter Vigil. Why is this an appropriate reading for that season of the Church year?

2. It is true that "God's saving power will inevitably conquer," and that "Those who erect their own ideas and plans into divinities, those who stand against God, will ultimately find their projects in ashes, their existence empty of true life and meaning." Can you identify one instance where this has proved true in your own life or in a well-known event of our times?

CHAPTER IV

YAHWEH OUR GOD MADE A COVENANT WITH US

ISRAEL STRUGGLES TO EXPRESS ITS RELATIONSHIP WITH GOD

Please read: Exodus 19-20

Israel was aware of a special relationship between itself and Yahweh. The experiences of history, as interpreted by men of faith, had taught them what their God was like. His stance toward them they believed they could express in these words: "If you hearken to my voice and keep my covenant, you shall be my special possession, dearer to me than all other people, though all the earth is mine. You shall be to me a kingdom of priests, a holy people" (Ex 19.5-6).

But how could Israel think through this experience and relationship? How could it contemplate all that was implied in this living contact with God?

Israel did what any group, or any individual, at any time, does. The world of ideas of its time furnished the material to express, to think about, to elaborate on, how people and God stood toward each other. The word and notion "covenant," in Hebrew *berith*, seemed to fit the God-Israel situation.

THE COVENANT FORM

The Near East, before Israel's liberation from slavery in Egypt and through the years thereafter, produced many agreements and treaties that are known as "covenants."

There are numerous treaties whose texts, or parts of them, still exist, and which include all or some of the components, which are set forth below.

There may be some terms and references that are not immediately understandable but the general sense will be clear. The purpose of introducing these texts is to indicate the kind of materials that biblical historians have available to work with.

A. *Preamble* — an introduction of the king who is imposing the treaty. One king, Mursilis, begins his treaty with another king in the following way:

"These are the words of the Sun Mursilis, the great king, the king of the Hatti land, the valiant, the favorite of the Storm-god, the son of Suppiluliumas, the great king of the Hatti land, the valiant."

B. *Historical Summary* — a statement of the past relationships that have existed between the two kings or their countries.

In the latter part of the fourteenth century, B. C., Mursilis continues by describing what has gone on between him and Duppi-Tessub, the exotically-named king on whom he is imposing his covenant.

"Aziras was the grandfather of you, Duppi-Tessub. He rebelled against my father, but submitted again to my father. When the kings of Nuhassi land and the kings of Kinza re-

belled against my father, Aziras did not rebel. As he was
bound by treaty,he remained bound by treaty . . .When . . .
I seated myself on the throne of my father, Aziras behaved
toward me as he had behaved toward my father . . .When
your father died, in accordance with your father's word I
did not drop you. Since your father had mentioned to me
your name with great praise, I sought after you. To be sure,
you were sick and ailing, but although you were ailing, I,
the Sun, put you in place of your father . . ."

Notice how even in this abbreviated version the past history of the two kings is spelled out. What is implied in this
recitation is that the king on whom the covenant is being
imposed ought to be grateful to the king imposing the
treaty for all he has done for him and his people. He will
thus be happy to serve that king. Furthermore, because of
the favors he has granted, the king imposing the covenant
has every right to demand service from the king with whom
he is covenanting.

C. *Stipulations* — the specific provisions of the covenant.
Some of the conditions that Mursilis presented to Duppi-
Tessub ran as follows:

". . .When you beget an heir, he shall be king . . . and
just as I shall be loyal toward you, even so shall I be loyal
toward your son. But you, Duppi-Tessub, remain loyal
toward the king of the Hatti land, the Hatti land, my sons
and my grandsons forever! The tribute which was imposed
upon your grandfather and your father —. . .300 shekels of
gold . . .—you shall present to them likewise . . .With my
friend you shall be friend, and with my enemy you shall
be enemy . . ."

D. *Deposit of Treaty* — often the treaty provided for placing
a copy in a temple before the statue of a god or goddess
who was the protector of the treaty and the avenger of
violations. One treaty reads:

"A duplicate of this tablet has been deposited before the Sun-goddess of Arinna, because the Sun-goddess of Arinna regulates kingship and queenship."

E. *Invocation of the Gods as Witnesses* – a litany of the gods and goddesses who are witnesses of the treaty. Again, a treaty reads in part:

"We have called the gods to be assembled and the gods of the contracting parties to be present, to listen and to serve as witnesses: The Sun-goddess of Arinna . . .The Sun-god, the lord of heaven, the Storm-god . . .the Patron-god of the field, the Patron-god of the shield . . .the warlike Ishtar . . . the Moon-god lord of the oath . . ."

F. *Curses and Blessings* – the good or evil called down for keeping or breaking the treaty. Mursilis takes care of Dubbi-Tessub in fine fashion:

"The words of the treaty and the oath that are inscribed on this tablet – should Duppi-Tessub not honor these words of the treaty and the oath, may these gods of the oath destroy Duppi-Tessub together with his person, his wife, his son, his grandson, his house, his land and together with everything he owns.

"But if Duppi-Tessub honors these words of the treaty and the oath that are inscribed on this tablet, may these gods of the oath protect him together with his person, his wife, his son, his grandson, his house and his country."

THE COVENANT FORM IN THE OLD TESTAMENT

This covenant idea and form which was part of the life of the Near East, is reflected in the Old Testament. Both the idea and the form are used to spell out the relationship between Yahweh and his people. A few examples are included here to illustrate the point.

A. *Preamble* — Yahweh introduces himself, or is introduced: "Thus says the LORD , the God of Israel . . ." (Jos 24.2) "Then God delivered all these commandments . . ." (Ex 20.1).

B. *Historical Summary* — a survey of what Yahweh has done for his people:

"I, the LORD, am your God, who brought you out of the land of Egypt, that place of slavery" (Ex 20.2).

". . .I brought your father Abraham from the region beyond the River and led him through the entire land of Canaan. I made his descendants numerous and gave him Isaac . . .Then I sent Moses and Aaron, and smote Egypt with the prodigies which I wrought in her midst. Afterward I led you out of Egypt . . ." (Jos 24. 2-13).

C. *Stipulations* — the provisions of the covenant with Yahweh.

Exodus 20.3-17 — The Ten Commandments

D. *Deposit of Treaty* in the presence of Yahweh.

In Deuteronomy 10, after Moses has been given the Ten Commandments inscribed on stone, he says, "I turned and came down the mountain, and placed the tablets in the ark I had made. There they have remained, in keeping with the command the LORD gave me."

The ark was a small chest kept in the Israelite sanctuary.

E. *Invocation of Gods as Witnesses* — since Israel worshiped only one God, Yahweh, this could not be part of its understanding of covenant. However, a related idea did operate.

In Joshua 24.27, after the people have renewed their covenant relationship with Yahweh, Joshua is reported to have set up a large stone and said, "This stone shall be our witness, for it has heard all the words which the Lord spoke to us. It shall be a witness against you, should you wish to deny your God."

F. *Curses and Blessings* — for observance or non-observance of the covenant: Deuteronomy 28 has a long list of comforting benefits and hair-raising evils that depend on the keeping of the covenant with Yahweh. The summary goes:

"If you continue to heed the voice of the LORD, your God, and are careful to observe all his commandments which I enjoin on you today, the LORD, your God, will raise you high above all the nations of the earth. When you hearken to the voice of the LORD, your God, all these blessings will come upon you and overwhelm you . . ."

"But if you do not hearken to the voice of the LORD, your God, and are not careful to observe all his commandments which I enjoin on you today, all these curses shall come upon you and overwhelm you . . ."

Not to lose sight of the main issue — all this explanation leads to a very important conclusion.

God seems to speak here in the language of the time. But how? Men are reflecting on their experience of and insights about him and are expressing that faith in language which is formed by the culture and set of ideas current at the time. This process, through faith, is understood — both then and now — to be directed and moved by God himself. When the process is properly understood, it is perfectly legitimate to refer to God "speaking."

This says a great deal about the understanding of God-language at any time. God surpasses the ability of the human mind to understand him and of any language to express him. If this were not true, God would not be God. Christians believe that the most perfect expression of God is to be found in Jesus Christ. However, even the truth

35

from and about Jesus has to be formulated in language dependent on time and culture. No generation, no school of theology, will ever capture totally all that God is. We will always need new words, new experiences to help us see more deeply into the reality of God. We will always be using biblical revelation and the insights of the theology of past generations of believers to evaluate the experience of the present. Then we will need the tools of current language and culture to put into words new appreciations of God.

BEYOND *BERITH*

The notion of covenant, certainly central in the Old Testament, itself illustrates the above principle. While Israel used "covenant" as one way to express its relationship with God, the covenant notion had to be adapted to fit the uniqueness of God.

Obviously, when used in reference to God, the direction is religious, not political. Yahweh is the Great King who demands undivided allegiance of mind and heart from those on whom he freely bestows his benefits.

Further, this covenant is not a treaty between equals or one of mutual convenience. The people have no claim on Yahweh, except that to which he commits himself. There is no instance of God indicating, "If you do such-and-such, then I will be obliged to give you so-and-so." If this were the situation, the covenant or agreement would be greater than God. What really happens is that God has acted as deliverer from Egypt of his own free will. He continues in a living, loving relationship to this particular group of people. The full meaning of this relationship, which may seem exclusive and arbitrary, will not be completely evident until it reaches its term in Jesus Christ who brings salvation for all men.

The Hebrew word that is commonly used to express Yahweh's relationship to his people is *hesed*. Very hard to translate, the word comes into English translations as "loving-kindness," "mercy," "fidelity," to mention only a few possibilities. It designates God's own commitment to the relationship that he has established with his people. He never forgets it, never puts it away. All his dealings with men are governed by what he is, a saving Presence.

The provisions of the covenant, the Ten Commandments, do not produce the relationship between God and his people. Rather, they are the expression of Israel's special relationship with God. An Israel faithful to the commandments is an Israel appreciating and responding to all that God has been for it. An Israel unfaithful to the commandments has turned its back on its Savior.

Finally, even this covenant idea is too feeble to capture the richness of God's commerce with his people. Other places in the Old Testament will use other images: God is husband, the people are his wife; God is father, the people are his son, and so on. And there are types of covenants or agreements between God and his people different from the one described above.

THE COVENANT

The concretizing of the God-Israel relationship in terms of covenant still casts welcome light in the darkness confronting modern man.

1. God reveals himself in his deeds. Because he loves, he breaks into history and through the dramas that work themselves out on its stage, "God in act" can be perceived. Of course, to stress this point once again, although signs of God's power, these acts seldom, if ever, carry inescapable proof in themselves that God's hand has caused them. Such actions, even the life, death and resurrection of Jesus

Christ, require spokesmen to interpret their meaning, and faith to accept that meaning.

2. God is not wilful, unreasonable, petulant, unknowable. He makes known what life is, what he is, what man is. He does this through a living association with a community of faith which he has chosen to know and serve him. Because God is consistent, trust and a sense of security about ultimate meaning and values are possible. Man need not wander the face of the earth lost and without guidance. God's meaning for life, which is the only meaning that counts, is available.

3. A response is expected of man, not because God needs it but because man does. The response, the keeping of God's way, is the only thing which insures that man will not be eternally frustrated in attaining his deepest yearnings.

4. Those who have faith, who do accept the reality of their relationship with God, should, by the quality of their lives and the faith explanation they give, become a challenge to the other values and interpretations of life current in their times.

SUGGESTIONS FOR REFLECTION

1. A covenant is an agreement or treaty that was different from a contract because it was imposed by a victor or king on another ruler. Because he had granted favors, the king imposing the covenant had every right to demand service from the ruler with whom he was covenanting. The Israelites saw this as one way of spelling out the relationship between Yahweh and his people. Why does the Church today sometimes express its relationship to God as a New Covenant?

2. Does the term, "Covenant," as used in this chapter, express adequately your relationship with God? How does the

covenant bind God? How does the covenant bind each person?

3. "I have always tried to live a decent life, but God has not rewarded me or always answered my prayers," a Catholic complained. How does this person's idea of God's commitment to him differ from the idea presented in a covenant?

4. Select the one of the following images of God from the Old Testament that you believe best expresses your relationship to him, and explain why:
God is king; the people are his vassals
God is husband; the people are his wife
God is father; the people are his son.

5. "God is not wilful, unreasonable, petulant, unknowable. He makes known what life is, what he is, what man is." How does this statement relate to the Ten Commandments? Where does faith enter into the explanation?

CHAPTER V

HEAR, O ISRAEL,
THE STATUTES AND DECREES

THE TEN COMMANDMENTS

Please read: Exodus 20. 1-17

"So there is something special between me and God.
What do I do about it?   How do I behave or react? "

The religious person, the one who experiences a relationship to a being beyond himself, can react in a number of
ways. He can be afraid with the dread of the unknown.
He can toy with superstition and magic, which are attempts
to control the Awesome Power by rituals and ceremonies
that will tame that Power and put it to one's own use.

Israel believed that its response to God came in the keeping of the Ten Laws, Ten Directions for Life, Ten Commandments.

The faith of Israel, and of Christians, holds that God gave
these commandments. Does that mean that God literally
dictated or wrote Ten Rules?   Do the directives in the commandments make their appearance without any preparation
or precedent in the history of mankind?

LAW IN THE NEAR EAST

"Law" becomes a necessity when people begin living together. Something has to control conduct as soon as a family has a neighbor. Too many areas of possible conflict develop. Can you park your bicycle in my driveway? If my tree hangs over your backyard, can you cut off its branches? If four of us drive our cars up to the four corners of a crossroad at the same time, who goes first?

In all these situations, law means some standard, socially acceptable way of dealing with the situations and somebody who can enforce the pattern of conduct. Otherwise, "might makes right" would probably be the Golden Rule.

The people of the Near East had laws. These developed out of life as it was then. They were intended to provide some kind of security in every-day living.

Laws were born from conflict or problem cases. These problems were settled by some authority figure: local chieftain, village headman, king. Once a decision was made, this decision became the precedent for other similar situations in the same place and elsewhere.

This is not so far removed from our own legal procedures. In handing down their decisions, our law courts will refer to the Case of X vs. Y in 1927 when a parallel case was adjudicated in such and such a way.

The lands of the Near East in the thirteenth century B. C. shared much in common. Agriculture, stock raising, commerce and trading were the ways of making a living. There were differences in culture, but there were many likenesses.

This common civilization gave rise to a common way of looking at life situations, and this common perspective gave rise to similar laws.

The laws were expressed in two forms. The much more common form is called *casuistic* law, i. e., a law which describes a particular case that needs solution, and then gives the solution. *Apodictic* law simply asserts "Do" or "Don't." "Thou shalt" and "Thou shalt not" are apodictic law.

Pardon what may seem like a dull and pedantic intrusion, but here are some laws from the Near East. The Old Testament can be understood only against its background, and the background can be understood only by some direct contact, however brief, with that background.

Around 1700 B. C., the king of Babylonia was named Hammurabi. A collection of laws he gathered was discovered early in our own century, with 282 articles covering a wide variety of life situations.

Suppose one person pokes out the eye of another. The Code of Hammurabi handles this case with different solutions depending on the social status of the one who had his eye poked out.

"If a citizen has destroyed the eye of one of citizen status, they shall destroy his eye."

"If he has destroyed the eye . . . of a vassal, he shall pay one mina of silver" (a sum of money).

"If he has destroyed the eye of a slave of a citizen, . . . he shall pay half of his market-value."

What about kidnapping? Hammurabi's Code specifies: "If a citizen steals the child of a citizen, he shall die."

Take something no longer common, a temperamental ox who likes to gore. What if he injures or kills somebody? The rules of Hammurabi covered this case also.

"If the offending ox belonged to a citizen who has been notified by the authorities of its propensity to gore, and he has not removed its horns, or has not tethered the ox, and that ox gored a man of citizen status occasioning his death, he shall pay a half-mina of silver."

Some things worth noticing about these laws are:
a. they are similar to other laws in other law codes found in the Near East;
b. they are "casuistic," i. e. they state a case and solve it;
c. they have different kinds of penalties depending on the social status of the offender and the one who is injured. The penalty is less for knocking out the eye of a vassal than for knocking out the eye of a citizen.

The point of all this is to prepare us to discover that the laws in the Old Testament very often reflect the same kind of problems, and sometimes the same solutions, as the laws of other people around Israel.

Suppose an Israelite hit a slave in such a way as to blind him in one eye. Exodus 21.26 states: "When a man strikes his male or female slave in the eye and destroys the eye, he shall let the slave go free in compensation for the eye."

Or kidnapping: "A kidnapper, whether he sells his victim or still has him when caught, shall be put to death" (21.16).

Or the nasty ox again: "When an ox gores a man or a woman to death, the ox must be stoned; its flesh may not be eaten. The owner of the ox, however, shall go unpunished. But if an ox was previously in the habit of goring people and its owner, though warned, would not keep it in; should it then kill a man or a woman, not only must the ox be stoned, but its owner also must be put to death. If, however, a fine is imposed on him, he must pay in ransom for his life whatever amount is imposed on him" (21.28-30).

All this suggests that when the Old Testament says that "God gave such and such a law or commandment to the Israelites," those laws and commandments might have already been part of the legal heritage of the people around Israel.

THE TEN COMMANDMENTS

But what about the Ten Commandments which have served as the basis for the Judaeo-Christian moral code for centuries? Are these unique? Or are these similar to standards put before the pagan neighbors of the Israelites?
Are the commandments revealed directly by God in a blinding flash of light, or are they the result of human thinking through social situations?

THE NEIGHBOR COMMANDMENTS

In the commands which control how the Israelite was to live with his fellow Israelite, there is nothing startlingly new. When compared with other laws of the period, they share a basic outlook on how one should deal with others.
Let us briefly consider the probable meaning each commandment originally had.

"Honor your father and your mother." This very likely had to do with aged parents. As their capacity for work diminished and they became economic liabilities, there might be a temptation for the children with whom they lived to make life unpleasant, to begrudge them food, to force them to leave the home, to push them to suicide, to kill them. (Interesting how the more things change, the more they stay the same). This command stood in the way of any such treatment, and in the course of time, took on even broader application.

"You shall not kill." There has been a great deal of discussion about the meaning of this law. Very likely, its original intent was against illegal killing. It protected against wanton murder, but was not an absolute prohibition

44

of capital punishment or of war. In fact, all through the Old Testament, both the death penalty and war are considered legitimate. Capital punishment is actually part of the law code here (21.12-14).

"You shall not commit adultery." This command was not concerned with "purity" or "chastity," but, strangely enough, with justice. This will be very unpalatable in these days of women's rights, but what was wrong with adultery was the violation of the husband's rights. His wife belonged to him. For another man to have intercourse with her was an unjustified use of his possession.

"You shall not steal." Although more speculative than some of the other statements made here, the common belief of scholars is that this command originally dealt with the kidnapping of a free Israelite man. No one was allowed to do this. The original object of "You shall not steal" was thus "a free Israelite man."

"You shall not bear false witness against your neighbor." The administration of law was not handled by well-trained prosecutors, defense attorneys and judges. The usual situation, at least in early times was for local leaders, not especially skilled in law, to make judgments. Since there was no possibility for all the safeguards of later legal systems, all the technical know-how, etc., everything depended on rigorous honesty on the part of witnesses. The outcome of a case hung upon the words of those who testified.

This command insisted upon absolute truthfulness in the law court. Whatever was said there was a public exposure of the reputation of one's neighbor.

"You shall not covet your neighbor's house. You shall not covet your neighbor's wife, nor his male or female slave, nor his ox or ass, nor anything else that belongs to him." The Hebrew word translated as "covet" refers to an inner feeling that, with a certain inevitability, leads to the cor-

responding action. The implication is that if I "covet" my neighbor's house, as sure as night follows day, I will make whatever moves necessary to get that house. What is forbidden is not so much an interior impulse as the practical results of that impulse which flow almost necessarily from it.

Originally, "You shall not steal" protected a man's liberty. "You shall not covet" protected everything else that was his.

THE GOD COMMANDMENTS

What about those commandments that regulate man's actions toward God?

"You shall not have other gods besides me." What did the Israelites at the time of Moses believe about their God? Was he the only God, or were there other gods besides Yahweh?

Monotheism involves a statement of belief in only one God, the absolute denial of all other gods, and the proposition that, since there is only one God, he must be God for all men, not for just one particular country or people.

Was Israel monotheistic from the very beginning? The answer has to be qualified by some further considerations of monotheism.

Suppose two young people are going steady. They go out only with each other. They spend most of their free time together. They enjoy each other's company immensely and can't wait for the times when they can be together. However, they have never explicitly talked about getting married. They're just caught up in what they're doing now and haven't looked too much to the future yet.

Then one day, a friend asks them, "Are you two planning to get married? " Perhaps they say, "Well, we really hadn't thought about it yet. But yes, it looks as if we will get married." Once this break-through happens, their plans become more explicit. They tell their families. They set the date and begin making arrangements. That they will be getting married is now clear for all to see.

Whether or not this example is real can be left for discussion. The important thing is to accept the story and see what has developed between the young man the the young woman.

They have gotten so close to one another that they simply begin behaving as if there were no one else in life for either of them. After they have lived this life style for a while, they make explicit what they have been living out. They belong to each other and will express that in marriage.

This gives some idea of the process that Israel went through. Explicit statements that there is only one God and no others do not come till the middle of the sixth century before Christ, in chapters 40-55 of the Book of Isaiah. These chapters from an anonymous prophet include professions of faith like:
"I am the first and I am the last,
    there is no God but me.
Who is like me?   Let him stand up and speak,
    make it evident, and confront me with it." (Is 44.6-7).
"I am the LORD and there is no other,
    there is no God besides me.
It is I who arm you, though you know me not,
    so that toward the rising and the setting of the sun
    men may know that there is none besides me"(Is 45.5-6).

Does the lateness of such explicit professions mean that Israel believed in many gods during the roughly 700 years that passed from Moses to these passages?

The kind of monotheism which directly rules out the existence of other gods is called *theoretical monotheism*. This is a carefully thought-through, explicitly stated position, much like the final statement of our young couple. They got to the point of saying, yes, the way they had been living was an indication that they intended to spend their lives together.

But that does not mean that they were not the only ones for each other long before they made that final, explicit declaration. Even before then, they were behaving as if they were the only ones for each other.

There is a parallel situation in religious practice which scholars call *practical monotheism*. This describes the attitude of people who have not yet made a specific statement, "there is only one God, no others." But for all practical purposes, they are behaving as if that were the case.

That was the way with Israel, at least from the time of Moses and the Ten Commandments. In the Ten Commandments and the life style of Israel, the emphasis was on total disregard for all gods but Yahweh. He acts wherever he pleases, even in lands which worship other gods. He is absolutely unique.

Because this is so, Israel must believe in and obey only this God, Yahweh. That is what is stated in the first commandment. Yahweh demands that he be worshiped exclusively. He is the only God worth the attention of Israel. He is the only God who counts. Next to him, all the other gods that people imagine or create pale into nothing.

Living according to this state of mind will eventually lead to the explicit statements in the chapters of Isaiah mentioned above, that not only do other gods not count, they do not even exist. The *only* God is Yahweh.

"You shall not carve idols for yourselves in the shape of anything in the sky above or on the earth below or in the waters beneath the earth; you shall not bow down before them or worship them."

In the religious thought of the Near East, the statue or image of the god was his dwelling place. Not so much the gross belief that the statue was the god, but the conviction that the divine being took up residence in the material and form of the representation.

However, from this, it can be only a short, easy skip to behaving as if possession and care of the statue gave those who cared for it control over the god whose presence resided in the statue or image. To put it another way, there was the danger that the image of the god would become a kind of magic machine to be operated for one's own benefit. Once the right words were recited, the right ritual performed, the right movements made to or for the image, then the divine power had to be released. The god was reduced to doing what the people wanted him to do.

This command forbids Israel to make images of its God. Yahweh is not like the pagan gods, to be manipulated by priests and functionaries. People do not control Yahweh. How can they since he is the Master and Lord of all the universe?

Furthermore, the heart of the religion of Israel was that Israel met God not in images and pictures but in his deeds in history. As the events of history were played out under the direction of Yahweh, and were interpreted for Israel by the words of those especially chosen by him, God's presence would be felt and understood. God would always remain "beyond," "the Other," "the Holy." But at the same time, he would be present to those who could see his saving presence in what he was doing in the events of human history.

"You shall not take the name of the Lord, your God, in vain." This command is very close in intent to the one against images. In the thought world from which it came, to know someone's name gave a certain power over that person. To use that name was to put into operation the power of the name.

If not in real life, at least in late-show crime movies of older vintage, we still hear commands like "Open up in the name of the Law! " Or in some period piece adventure, the fleeing hero might try to get refuge from his pursuing enemies at the little cottage in the forest with a plea like, "In the name of God, hide me! "

These are suggestive of the use of the name in Old Testament times. Somehow, to use the name of "Law" or "God" brings to bear the authority of whatever is behind the name.

In pagan religions, in magic and sorcery, the names of gods were woven into rituals and incantations. The one invoking the name or names of gods theoretically forced the god to respond, to do what the suppliant wanted done.

This command for Israel again emphasized the reality that Yahweh is controlled by no one, by no ritual, by no magic, by no sorcery. He is supremely free. He is supremely in control. He makes himself present to his people, but on his terms. No one can demand anything from him as if due. No one can set up a situation in such a way that God has to respond or act along the lines devised by some human manipulator.

"Remember to keep holy the sabbath day." Where specifically the sabbath originated is very obscure. What is certain is that ancient custom almost universally observed a day of rest at certain intervals. In Israel this day took on a religious meaning special to itself. As a day for resting, a day for visiting the sacred shrines, the sabbath became an expression

of the covenant between Yahweh and Israel.

THE MEANING OF THE TEN COMMANDMENTS

Where does this investigation into the background and probable original meaning of the ever-present Ten Commandments leave us?

1. The commandments relating to one's neighbor bring nothing new as far as content goes to the legal custom of the other people living around Israel. There is a certain deeper humaneness, a more profound respect for life in Israel's laws. There is a greater consideration for the slave who is treated as more than a piece of property. There is more pervasive equality. Class distinctions are minimized. Crimes are not considered more or less serious depending on the status of the one who commits the crime and the one who is the victim.

2. The introduction, "I, the LORD, am your God, who brought you out of the land of Egypt, that place of slavery," and the commandments that deal with Yahweh are special to Israel. The introduction states the special character of the relationship of Yahweh to Israel, his concern and presence for them, because of which they owe him obedience. That obedience demanded something unique in the law of the Near East, that Israel worship Yahweh only, that it recognize him as the Supreme One, the Only God deserving of attention and respect. That obedience also demanded that Israel recognize that it too stood under the power of God. It must not foolishly try to manipulate that power to its own purposes by the use of images and the Name of Yahweh. In other words, God was not the weapon of Israel for its national ambitions. Israel was the instrument of God for his purposes — and faith understood that those purposes were saving and good.

3. Very significant was the fact that the laws, even those

which governed the dealings with neighbors, were understood
as the working out of the relationship to God. The God-
to-man relationship took form not only in the ceremonies
of ritual, or in the quiet of man's personal prayers to God,
but in the way that one person lived with another. God
was concerned with more than what went on in the Holy
Place at Holy Times. God was concerned with everything
that filled life.

DID MOSES WRITE THE LAW?

The first five Books of the Bible contain chapter after
chapter of law, governing all types of activities. These
are presented as the commands of God given through or
by Moses. Is this an oversimplification?

Moses is "law-giver" in the sense of welding the people
into one by giving a common system of law a new meaning.
Through Moses, laws the Israelites knew and had already
been keeping took on deep significance. Observance of
the laws was the concrete manifestation of their faith in
Yahweh, the God who had freed them from Egypt.

Very likely Moses formulated a set of commands, Ten Commandments. Among these, the four regulations governing
attitudes toward Yahweh would have been basic. Through
these the rest of the commands got their force as the lived
expression of acknowledging Yahweh only.

There is no doubt, however, that the large collections of
laws in the Pentateuch do not come from the same person
at the same time in the same place. They are an accumu-
lation of laws from over the centuries developed to deal
with changing situations. For example, in Exodus 20.10,
the command to keep the sabbath states, "No work may be
done then either by you, or your son or daughter, or your
male or female slave, or your beast, or by the alien who
lives with you." This command makes sense only later

when the Israelites *are* prosperous enough to have slaves and animals of their own, and have their own homeland in which foreigners are dwelling. This did not happen until many years had passed after the Exodus.

Israel believed that the commands of God were alive. They had to be interpreted and adapted to new life situations if they were not to become dead words. Israel's leaders faced new situations, reflected on them in the light of the commands and customs they had inherited from the past, and made decisions about how to live in the here and now. And they felt perfectly justified in saying that all of this was the "word of Yahweh" because it was Yahweh who was directing them in their new way of life. They were alive and God was alive, and their living relationship to one another needed to be reflected on and re-expressed continuously.

THE TEN COMMANDMENTS TODAY

The Ten Commandments provide three of the four requirements for the traditional wedding ensemble for a bride.

There is something *old,* an acceptance of laws and customs in existence long before Israel formally came on the scene.

There is something *borrowed.* Many of the "do's" and "don'ts" were the accepted life styles of different peoples around the Israelites. These, as reflecting a common culture and civilization, became part of the law of Israel.

But there is definitely something *new.* That newness lies in considering the laws as more than a safeguard against a dog-eat-dog existence. The novelty was in the idea that God was concerned with what men did to one another.

One of the most authentic ways of demonstrating faith in Yahweh was behavior in everyday life. The Ten Commandments, and all the vast network of accompanying laws developed over centuries, amounted to a concrete and specific spelling out of the first commandment of Israel which was unique to itself: "I, the LORD, am your God . . . you shall not have other gods besides me."

There is much to be learned from this.

A. "God spoke" or "God said" does not necessarily mean an actual voice thundering among awed hearers. God can also speak through the customs and way of life that experience and reflection lead to.

B. Not everything that happens, however, not all customs, not all developments are from God. Since this is so, what is needed is some person, some community, guided by God, to help discern in which situations God is truly present, in which events the life and teaching of God is truly reflected. Moses was such a person. Guided by Yahweh, he formulated a way of life expressed in commandments and placed this before his contemporaries as God's will for them. Some of these commandments were the common culture of the day; some were not.

C. There is no way to *prove* that the commandments are from God, that Moses is from God. Despite centuries of study which have advanced biblical studies, despite impassioned sermons, despite all kinds of religious persons and experiences, whether one is willing to accept God's word still depends on faith, on the willingness to trust in God's presence here or there.

D. The Ten Commandments make a basic statement about God and man.

God is absolutely unique, the Lord of the Universe. All life comes from and leads to him. Man is a fool if he believes that God can be made into the instrument of personal or national aggrandizement. God expects obedience from man, not vice versa. But obedience to God is not bowing to the whims of a petty tyrant. It is the free embracing of a way that leads to life and salvation.

The commandments about man affirm human rights and dignities. Man has a right to life ("You shall not kill"); to liberty ("You shall not steal a fellow Israelite"); to the pursuit of happiness (in so far as this depends on the legitimate ownership of the goods of the world), to reputation ("You shall not bear false witness against your neighbor").

These statements about God and man are inseparable. There is no true relationship to God without a special kind of relationship to one's own brother.

E. Two important further considerations fill out the picture.

First, the commandments need to be made alive and pertinent to changing society and situations. The responsibility remains constant to try to determine what a single-minded commitment to the one, true God means in each day and age. No society can simply mouth the words of the past without trying to understand the implications of those words for its own circumstances. Each society must be in contact with the living God to hear his word for the here and now. And being in contact means knowing the traditions, of which the Scriptures form a foundation.

Second, the teaching of Jesus has brought us further than the Ten Commandments. 'You shall love the Lord your God with your whole heart, with your whole soul, and with all your mind.' This is the greatest and first commandment. The second is like it: 'You shall love your neighbor as yourself.' On these two commandments the whole law is based, and the prophets as well."

As the tradition did before him, Jesus tied love of God to love of neighbor. But he moved in a new direction when he broadened the concept of love of neighbor to include not just fellow Israelites, but all men, including enemies.

A NOTE ON THE NUMBERING OF THE COMMANDMENTS

I have avoided calling the commandments the first, the second, etc. The reason is that there is a different system of numbering for Catholics on the one hand, and for the general Protestant-Jewish tradition on the other.

The Ten Commandments are listed in two places, Exodus 20.1-17 and Deuteronomy 5.6-21.

The Catholic usage is to treat as one commandment, "You shall not have other gods besides me. You shall not carve idols for yourselves . . ." "You shall not covet your neighbor's house" and "You shall not covet your neighbor's wife" are arranged as two separate commands. (Notice Deuteronomy 5.21 with the command against coveting wife first, and then a listing of the neighbor's "goods," which are not to be coveted. This is the origin of the wording familiar to Catholics).

The Protestant-Jewish usage considers "You shall not have other gods besides me" and "You shall not carve idols" as independent commands. Then, the prohibition against coveting neighbor's goods and wife becomes one command.

In schematic form, the number differences turn out like this:

	Protestant-Jewish	Catholic
1st	no other gods	1st
2nd	no carved idols	1st
3rd	not use name in vain	2nd
4th	sabbath observance	3rd
5th	honor father and mother	4th
6th	not kill	5th

	Protestant-Jewish	*Catholic*
7th	not commit adultery	6th
8th	not steal	7th
9th	not bear false witness	8th
10th	not covet neighbor's wife	9th
	not covet neighbor's goods	10th

SUGGESTIONS FOR REFLECTION

1. Sometimes people attempt to control God's "awesome power by rituals and ceremonies that will tame that power and put it to their own use." Can you think of ways some people try to do this today?

2. Are commandments revealed directly by God in a blind - ing flash of light, or can they be the result of human thinking through social situations? Which is more likely in the human experience of laws? If the second were true, would it imply less power of God?

3. Select one of the "neighbor commandments" and try to imagine what the effect on life in the United States would be if this were eliminated as a commandment.

4. Reflect on the meanings of the three God-commandments and select the one that you think is in most need of being reiterated in our culture and times. Give your reasons. Which one of the three is most abused today? How do you celebrate a day of rest, a "Lord's Day" in your home?

5. The Ten Commandments are sometimes thought of as "saving acts." How can this be explained?

6. "Israel believed that the commands of God were alive. They had to be interpreted and adapted to new life situations if they were not to become dead words." How has our interpretation and adaptation of the commandments changed since the days of the Old Testament?

7. "The Ten Commandments make a basic statement about God and man." What do they tell you of God? What do they tell you of man? What further insights does Jesus give into their meaning in the relationship between God and man?

8. Mention at least one new insight you received from reading this chapter about the Ten Commandments.

9. Select the commandment with which you have the greatest personal difficulty. Change it to the opposite, or a positive focus (when the statement is negative), and make it the basis for your personal action during the month ahead. For example:
Thou shalt not kill . . .You shall be a life-giver and promoter
Thou shalt not steal . . .You shall share your possessions generously with your fellow men, etc.

CHAPTER VI

I WILL MAKE OF YOU
A GREAT NATION

ABRAHAM THE ANCESTOR

It may seem strange that we are moving backwards. We began our considerations with the Exodus, an event that took place sometime about 1250 B. C. Now we move back five hundred or more years, to about 1800 B. C., to the man Israelites revered as their ancestor.

Why this way of proceeding? The liberation from Egypt, seen with faith, is the heart of the belief of Israel. The Exodus showed in a striking way the relationship of Yahweh with Israel. The commandments and laws which expressed Israel's response gave identity to Israel as a people. Israel really began to exist with the Exodus. From then on, it had a vantage point from which to look back on its history. It collected stories of heroes and leaders, traditions of past events, earlier religious expressions. All of this was seen in a new light as part of God's activity in making Israel his people.

WHAT WAS GOING ON

As indicated already, the Abraham traditions take us back to about 1800 B. C. — the date can vary by a century or so in either direction.

The Israelites looked to Mesopotamia as the place of their origin. We have already seen that when they are described as "Hebrews," the term refers not to nationality or race but to social condition. Hebrews were people without official status. For various reasons, they did not own property or enjoy the rights of free citizens in the lands where they lived. Generally, they kept apart from the densely settled areas in those countries within whose boundaries they took up residence. Often they supported themselves as soldiers, or migrant workers. Sometimes, as in Egypt, they were put to forced labor. One scholar holds that for expressing the social and legal status of Hebrews at this time, "tramp" is a legitimate English equivalent, if this means someone who lives apart from the general population centers and earns what he needs by doing odd jobs, while keeping a freedom of movement from place to place. Another believes that the evidence indicates that many of these Hebrews were occupied in operating the large donkey caravans that carried all kinds of products from one land to another.

Between the years 2000 and 1500 B. C., there were large-scale migrations from east to west in Mesopotamia. As pressure was put on one group of people to move westward, these in turn pushed out the inhabitants of the lands into which they had squeezed, and so on like a row of dominoes. The Hebrews were part of these migrations, and this restless movement forms the backdrop for the stories about Abraham.

One difference should be noted between the Hebrews generally and Abraham and his line. The latter seem to be on a higher social and economic level. Abraham, Isaac and Jacob emerge from the pages of Genesis as in process of settling down. They own flocks. They are small scale farmers gradually growing prosperous.

"ABRAHAM, GET UP AND MOVE"

Please read: Genesis 12

To anticipate slightly, the story of Abraham, the ancestor of the Israelites, as Genesis now tells it, is not an isolated incident preserved for the sake of curiosity or even historical information. In the large plan of Genesis, the first eleven chapters are the story of evil and its festering spread. Genesis 1-11 creates a dreary and hopeless picture — of sin spoiling man's relationship with God, with man and with all creation. There seems no possibility for things ever to get better. Evil grows and grows and man is ever more painfully trapped under its weight. This will be the topic of the next chapters. For now, suffice it to say that at this point of despair and dejection, the Israelites saw the meaning and purpose of Abraham.

While man can do nothing to pull himself out of the claws of evil, God can. God begins that centuries-lasting process with his call to a man, a Hebrew, named Abraham.

There is no previous indication that God was preparing to intervene in the way that he did, in the sordid, sin-riddled history of man. The story simply begins, "The Lord said to Abram: Go forth . . .to a land that I will show you . . . I will make of you a great nation . . .All the communities of the earth shall find blessing in you."

Nothing in the story explains God's call. It is simply God's free action to begin to be the Liberator that he is. From all the peoples and all the nations, God chooses — for his own good reasons — Abraham. From him salvation will come and through him all "communities of the earth shall find blessing."

"Blessing" generally carries the meaning of an abundant life. This includes possessions, numerous children, and the assurance that the line of descendants will go on far into the future. This concept of what constitutes blessing and happiness does not indicate a pre-occupation with material things for their own sake to the exclusion of "spiritual" values. For Israel, God was life. Since the idea of an after-life which is at all worth while does not develop till much later, the signs of being tied into God's life had to appear strong and clear right now. The most obvious sign of being close to the goodness, greatness, power of God was life bursting with an abundance of all good things.

Abraham is chosen to be the one through whom God's blessings come to men. The history that finds expression in the Bible will be a growth in the understanding of the full content of that blessing.

THE "HISTORY" OF ABRAHAM

A final item to keep in mind as the stories of Abraham unfold: the Israelites did not have Abraham's diary, or his notebooks, or his autobiography, or even a biography written by someone close to him. They did have traditions about where they came from, about their ancestors. They had their faith in Yahweh as working for them and control-ling their history. All these went into a portrait of Abraham conditioned by faith, or better, several portraits. J, E and P are very much in evidence in the Genesis story of Abraham, or Abram, as he was then named.

GOD'S PROMISE THREATENED

Genesis 12 brings Abraham to the land of Canaan where a famine develops. Abraham goes down to Egypt, one of the breadbaskets of the Near East, where the water of the Nile ensured a regular food supply.

Then comes a curious story. Abraham fears that the Egyp-tians, and particularly the Pharaoh, will be taken by the beauty of Sarah, or Sarai, his wife. Desirous of her, they might simply eliminate Abraham, the alien without rights, by murder. Abraham instructs Sarah to tell the Egyptians that she is his sister rather than his wife. She follows instructions when, sure enough, her beauty causes so much of a stir that she is taken into Pharaoh's palace. Abraham does well as a result. The Egyptians give flocks and slaves to the fortunate brother of so lovely a lady.

But then some kind of plagues torment Pharaoh's household. Through these, he learns that Sarah is really the wife of Abraham. Pharaoh reproves Abraham for the deceit and sends Sarah back.

The background of this unusual tale is worthy of comment. It shows how ancient traditions were preserved by the Israelites, even when they were no longer quite sure what the traditions meant.

Many laws from lands from which the Israelites believed they emigrated have been found. One such law indicates a peculiar situation in marriage. The bonds of marriage were considered strongest and most solemn if the wife also had the status of sister to her husband. No matter what the actual blood ties were, a man could marry and then also adopt his wife as his sister. Such a wife-sister had a higher status than a wife not adopted as sister. The wife-sister position was highly cherished. At least one of the points of the arrangement, legal fiction though it was, was that the children born of a brother and sister were guaranteed a pure blood strain. The family blood was not being mixed because the children were conceived and born from the same line.

This arrangement, reaching far back into the past, was very likely no longer understood by Israel. So, even though it preserved the story of the custom, and historical research has shown that the memory was an accurate one, Israel no longer knew what it meant. In the course of time, it gave the story a new meaning that had a theological purpose.

Abraham had been promised descendants and a land.
Throughout his story in Genesis, that promise was threatened
and attacked. The experiences of Abraham and Sarah, especially with the Pharaoh, are such a threat.

First of all, the famine is a threat. If Abraham and Sarah
stay in Canaan, they may perish through starvation. Finis
for the promise of descendants and homeland.

If they move down to Egypt, they will be leaving the land
of promise for a foreign country. Again, finis for the promise.

In the story, Abraham opts to go to Egypt, which will at
least offer the hope of survival.

But hardly have the couple escaped one danger, famine,
than another threatens. Pharaoh is captivated by Sarah and
takes her into his harem. How can Abraham become the
founder of a great nation, if he doesn't even have a wife to
begin a family?

God intervenes. He brings misfortune on the household of
Pharaoh which makes Pharaoh understand that he is doing
something wrong. He sends Sarah back to Abraham and the
possibility of the promise being fulfilled goes on.

A secondary issue is the, to us, peculiar morality. Abraham
lies about his wife. Pharaoh is punished even though he is
absolutely guiltless. He has taken Abraham at his word that
Sarah is his sister. For this he suffers.

But personal morality is not at all the issue. The incident
is not intended to portray norms of conduct, standards of
right and wrong, except in one area.

The spotlight is on Yahweh. The promise of God is threatened. Yahweh intervenes in what is going on to make sure that the promise will not come to a dead end. The lesson is the power of God, who is faithful to his word.

ABRAHAM TRIES THINGS HIS WAY

Please read: Genesis 15

Abraham's story continues with a very shrewd bit of planning on his part.

Time has passed and still no child has been born to carry on the line of Abraham, to be the living sign of God's promise. Abraham reasons that perhaps he ought to take matters into his own hands. If he cannot have a natural son, he will adopt one. He proposes that this adopted son be his heir, the one in whom God's promise will live on.

Yahweh's answer is "No! " "Look up at the sky and count the stars, if you can. Just so shall your descendants be." "Abram put his faith in the LORD, who credited it to him as an act of righteousness."

Abraham is to wait, to leave everything to God.

As a reminder of God's promise, an ancient ritual for making treaties comes into operation. A number of birds and animals are killed, the animals split in half and then arranged opposite each other in two rows. Fire, a symbol of God, makes a blazing passage down the row.

The original ceremony was a treaty ritual, like smoking a peace pipe or heads of state signing an agreement with diplomats standing round and TV cameras focused on them. The two parties making the treaty walked between the butchered animals; the meaning was that the fate of the animals should be their own if they were unfaithful to the agreement.

In this story, God is depicted as fitting himself to the ways of man. The Lord, in the form of fire, passes between the bloody carcasses to impress on Abraham God's fidelity to his word. Abraham is asked to do nothing because this treaty is not a matter of tit-for-tat. It is God's free binding of himself to his people.

ABRAHAM TRIES AGAIN

Please read Genesis 16 (and Genesis 21, another version of the same incident)

Abraham and Sarah grow older and still there is no sign of the promised son. Sarah suggests that Abraham father a son by Hagar, Sarah's Egyptian slave girl. Abraham is agreeable. Hagar conceives.

As will happen, what seemed like a solution turns out to be a problem. Hagar gives Sarah a bad time because she has been able to give Abraham the child that Sarah could not. Sarah fights back, abusing Hagar so much that the wretched girl runs away. In the wilderness, God's messenger tells her to return. She does, and at the home of Abraham bears the boy, Ishmael.

Disconcerting morality? Perhaps for us. But research has shown that what is described here fits in very well with the customs of the period.

Law codes of the time contain statutes providing that a childless wife is to furnish a female slave for her husband so that he might have sons. This had nothing to do with adultery or some other aspect of sexual morality. The concern is for the continuation and increase of the family. If the wife is barren, other steps can, and must, be taken.

The story takes us again into the authentic background of the times.

But there is an added complication. Within this chapter, there is a literary form called an *etiology*. An etiology is, simply put, the explanation of something in the present by something that happened or is believed to have happened in the past.

Here is a personal example.

I grew up in a small town with large areas of woodland on all sides. At the northwest section of the town, paths were plowed through the woodland to serve as fire-breaks and roads for fire equipment during brush fires. Because of the appearance this area took on — wide dirt paths separating rectangular stands of scrub oak and pine — it became known as "the squares." For years, old-time residents knew the section only by that name.

However, time was passing. The woodland gave way to housing developments, to a large school. The venerable fire lines disappeared. Yet old-timers still spoke about the newcomers who had moved into "the squares." When the newcomers learned that they were living in "the squares," they demanded explanations. There was nothing left to justify the name.

The newcomer asks, "Why is this section called 'the squares'? " The oldtimer answers, "Because . . ." and gives the explanation. This is an etiology.

Sometimes etiologies reflect what really happened, as in the above example. Sometimes the explanations given are fanciful.

Near "the squares" is a lake named Ronkonkoma, an Indian word. More imaginative interpretations of the name have been popular in some circles.

According to one, an Indian made the imprudent decision to go out on the lake in his canoe after having imbibed too

much of the white man's liquor. Canoeing can be tricky.
When the Indian got out into the middle of the lake, he
lost his balance, tipped the canoe and fell into the water.
Because of his condition, he could not make it back to
shore. Just before he went under for the third time, he
shouted "Rum conquered me! " Since his English was not
good, or poorly heard at the shore, it came over as "Ron
Konka Ma" or Ronkonkoma. Hence, the name — which
is pure imagination.

The justification for this local color is that etiologies play
a large part in the Old Testament. Sometimes these explanations have an historical core of truth. Sometimes they
are purely imaginative. And sometimes they are made up
on the basis of a present situation which is read back into
the past.

A double etiology is given for Ishmael, the name of Hagar's
son. Literally translated, Ishmael means "El (God) hears."
Hence, "You are now pregnant and shall bear a son; you
shall name him Ishmael. For the Lord has heard you, God
has answered you."

But there is more. Elsewhere in the Old Testament, the
Ishmaelites appear as a nomadic desert tribe. Like other
such tribes, they were raiders conducting hit-and-run at-
tacks on their more prosperous neighbors. The description
of Ishmael given here is really a description of a tribe that
bears his name. "He shall be a wild ass of a man, his hand
against everyone, and everyone's hand against him; in op-
position to all his kin shall he encamp."

This description of Ishmael very likely comes from the real
life experiences or memories that the Israelites had of a
tribe called Ishmaelites. It is read back to an individual
considered the ancestor-founder of the tribe.

This etiology business doesn't convey any especially deep
religious lesson but it does help to understand the frequent

statements in the Old Testament like "and because of this, the place is called X to this day." Or, "and because of this, the child was named Y."

Chapter 16 has ancient, dimly-remembered customs, moral views objectionable to us, folk-like explanations of names and people. Is there a lesson for life from God?

In the working out of Genesis, we must once more face here the power of God. A new element of suspense enters into the history of the promise. Abraham and Sarah still have no child. Sarah is barren. God's promise seems to be an empty word. Abraham tries to help God's plan along. If he has a son by the slave-girl, by a legal arrangement, this son will be his heir. God's word will then live on in that son.

Yahweh will have none of this. Human ingenuity is not the way to preserve and carry on God's plan. He will work out his own plan in his own time and in his own way. What he demands of Abraham is trust in him, although the reasons for trusting seem to be getting weaker and weaker as life slips away for the aged couple.

The lesson is clear for us: the need for trust in God and in his promise to be faithful to what he has declared through Jesus. At times, the teaching of the Scriptures will emphasize the role of men and women in carrying out God's plan. In the case of Abraham, all depends on God, who sees to it that his work goes on despite apparent failure. How he works is often incomprehensible to those standing at a single moment of time, but that is what must be learned.

THE SON IS BORN AND WHAT COMES NEXT

Please read: Genesis 21. 1-8; 22. 1-19

After perils, threats and challenges to the promise from many quarters, the long-expected son finally arrives, and this despite the fact that Abraham is old and Sarah long past the age for bearing children.

This joyous moment is followed in chapter 22 by a difficult, even repugnant, story. Abraham is ordered by God to slay his own son as a sacrifice.

Think of it! Abraham and Sarah have gone through the long years of waiting for this son. When things had gotten to the stage where his birth seemed impossible, he was born. Now that he has grown, the Lord gives the order to offer the boy as a sacrifice. This kind of God is almost enough to keep one from reading any further.

But there is more here than first meets the eye. The story begins with these words: "Some time after these events, God put Abraham to the test." This introduction lets the reader in on the secret from the beginning. What is going to happen is to show the depth of the faith of Abraham rather than to show a God who requires human killing as a gift to himself.

As the story is worked into the Genesis narrative of Abraham, this event is the climax of Abraham's life. What God asks of him is not simply obedience but the recognition that the promise, as it has taken shape in Isaac, is a pure gift of God. As gift, Abraham has no right to it. He cannot demand anything of God, not even that he keep his son.

Fortunately, as the story itself makes clear, God is not fickle and arbitrary, changing his mind, playing with the deepest emotions of humans. Even in the story, he had no intention of allowing Isaac to die. When Abraham demonstrates the depth of his trust in God, God renews the blessing he had promised — descendants "as countless as the stars of the sky and the sands of the seashore . . .in your descendants all the nations of the earth shall find blessing — all this because you obeyed my command."

This story is a legend, i. e. a narrative aiming to edify future generations by emphasizing the virtues of the main character. The point of the story is Abraham's obedience which is the example for all.

SUMMING UP ABOUT ABRAHAM: DID HE REALLY EXIST?

In the words of the famous scholar, Roland DeVaux: "We will never be in a position to write a historical biography of Abraham, Isaac, or Jacob, or even to write properly a history of the patriarchal period. We will always lack the necessary elements; even those which we have, inside and outside the Bible, show that the origins and the formation of Israel as a people were extremely complicated."

While not proving that Abraham existed, historical research has filled in the background from which Israel's ancestors came. The kind of social class to which Abraham belonged, the kind of life he led, the customs of his time, some of these are clearer now because of what research has uncovered of the laws, the customs, the history.

Israel believed it took its origins out of the countless thousands of people who plodded across the Near East in migrations and mass movements lasting over several hundred years. It remembered the name of one it considered its ancestor and preserved traditions about him. These it wove into its national history, which was a saga of a people and its God.

SUMMING UP ABOUT ABRAHAM: THE LESSON OF HIS LIFE AS GENESIS TELLS IT

Israel did pass on a view of God and life. God did not abandon man who had been dragged into the morass of sin and evil. God reached out to lift man from the trap. The total liberation would not happen all at once but through a long process in man's history and his understanding of

71

that history. It was to begin with the choice of a man, a family, caught in the restless movements of Near Eastern people. Israel's faith believed that to this man, to this family God made a promise. The promise was that the family would continue and grow, that it would settle in its own land, that through it the blessings of God would come on all the nations of the world.

How this would happen, what the blessing would be, still remained to be seen. What was demanded was trust in God, a willingness to throw oneself in with the way of life that he was offering, even if the final stages of this life remained out of sight. It meant realizing that no man could find by himself what this life was all about, much less reach it.

Abraham and his family trusted in God. Genesis tells a number of stories about this trust. Abraham left his own land. He learned more about trust through the failure of the various practical but overly human solutions he improvised to ensure the fulfillment of the promise. He showed his trust heroically and splendidly in the incident of the sacrifice of Isaac.

Now we know more of the plan of God. We know the salvation and freedom he offers through Jesus Christ. But we still need the faith, the trust of Abraham. We need to be willing to pick up and move after God, to put aside the various human solutions that are offered all around us as the meaning of life, to be willing to follow where God leads us because we trust him as our loving Father.

SUGGESTIONS FOR REFLECTION

1. In the story of Abraham, the fulfillment of the promise was threatened severely several times, so that it seemed a near impossibility. As you think of your life story of faith, can you identify setbacks or circumstances that seemed likely to prevent the fulfillment of its promise? Can you also identify ways in which, through it all, God was faithful to his promise?

2. God's own free initiative is the key point in Abraham's call, and in the making of the covenant with Abraham. Abraham did nothing previously to deserve or merit God's favor. Have you ever experienced a definite sign of God's taking the initiative in your life?

3. Have you ever tried unsuccessfully to manipulate events so that they would work out the way that you thought they should?

4. At times, it is very difficult to trust in God, especially as events seem to be militating against trust. Can you think of any time in history or in your own life when radical trusting in him proved to be the only answer?

5. Sometimes parents are very possessive of their children, acting as though they alone are responsible for their off-springs' past, present and future. How does the story of Abraham and Isaac throw new light on this relationship between parents and children?

6. As you are right now in the present, looking toward your own future, do you have a need for radical trust in God? Take a few moments to reflect on this, and to pray over it.

CHAPTER VII

"IN THE BEGINNING"—HOW IT ALL CAME TO BE

Please read: Genesis 1. 1-2. 4a

The story of creation is not a quaintly primitive relic of the past. It is a very highly polished theological presentation. The worst disservice we could do would be to ignore that fact and take it as a literal scientific or historical description.

THE HISTORICAL BACKGROUND

The important time element is not the date of creation, which the Bible in no way determines, but the time when this story about creation took shape. We shall reflect upon that time rather than upon the mysterious period of creation.

The verses you have been asked to read are from the P account, which means they were finally set together in the sixth or fifth century B. C. The story was not thought up then, but it was put into final form then.

What were those days like? Very difficult for Israel. The Israelites had lost their homeland to foreign conquerors and many of them had been dragged off into exile in an alien country. There the exiles met a new and impressive religion of many gods. These gods were splendidly honored in magnificent temples.

The deportees must have been sorely tempted. These new gods around them must have seemed strong and powerful.

After all, they ruled rich and prosperous lands. Yahweh's land had been overrun by their followers. These gods had beautiful houses for worship. The House of Yahweh in Jerusalem was a pile of rubble, razed by enemy armies.

In the face of such temptations, exiled priests gathered and shaped old traditions which affirmed in no uncertain terms that, no matter what, there was only one God, Yahweh, the God of Israel.

THE RELIGIOUS BACKGROUND

The Israelites were not the only people who puzzled about the beginnings of man, the world, the universe. Who am I? Where do I come from? What is life all about?

Man has always raised these questions as we can see from the records of his thoughts.

One of the stories of creation from the Near East is called the *Enuma Elish Epic.* All indications point to an original of this story from sometime around 2000 B. C.

The Enuma Elish Epic tells of the god, Apsu, and the goddess, Tiamat, who brought forth the other gods and goddesses. But not all was heavenly bliss in the land of gods and goddesses and a quarrel broke out. The conflict became so bitter that the goddess, Tiamat, was killed by a god named Marduk.

Marduk took the body of the goddess, split it in half, arched up half as the sky wherein he placed sun and moon, stars and constellations. The other half he pressed down as earth. Lo, the universe!

The gods who were allies of the slain Tiamat complained that they were being made slaves by the victorious gods on the side of Marduk. From now on, they would have to work with no hope of their toil ever ending.

The sympathetic Marduk listened to their pleas. He killed a rebel god and from his blood created man. Man was made to do the work that would otherwise have been laid on the gods.

Impatient with this story? Probably, because we live in different times, with different ways of expressing things. But this is *myth*. There are a great many definitions of myth. A simple one which will serve our purposes is that myth is an attempt to explain those things which are beyond the understanding of, more powerful than, out of the reach of, humans in terms humans can grasp and put into the language available.

In other words, to speak mythologically is to speak of powers which man recognizes as greater than himself. But if man is not to be reduced to silence about these mysteries, he must use his own limited language. The language never fits the reality totally.

Myth is not falsehood. Myth is an attempt to explain the ultimates in life. Myth is false only if the meaning in the myth is untrue.

There is no way of living without myth. No time in history, no generation, no matter how sophisticated, can formulate a language that will adequately express whatever life and power beyond himself man believes in.

There is no need here to go into a full explanation of how Enuma Elish looks at life. Enough to notice:
1. that the origin of all things is placed in primeval waters, in the chaos of the sea;
2. that the universe is created from the war between contesting gods or powers;
3. that the view of man is ambivalent, but with a definite pessimistic slant. Created from the blood of a god, his destiny from creation is to labor so that the gods might be released from labor. This view of man is echoed in the

Atra-hasis Epic, which dates back in written form to c. 1650 B. C.

THE SCIENTIFIC BACKGROUND

Perhaps science is not the right word. Whatever the right word, the focus is on the views of the universe that prevailed at the time. These emerge from a careful reading of literature of the period we are talking about, including Genesis itself and Enuma Elish.

The components of the universe were presumed to be what they looked like. This is what is called in some commentaries on the Scriptures, "science according to appearances." The earth, to one gazing around himself, who has had no great travel experience and has no sophisticated scientific instruments, looks like a relatively flat surface, with some mountainous elevations.   Oceans surge around the large land masses. A reasonable explanation is that the flat earth is like a pancake floating on the water of the oceans. Other water from underneath the earth seeps through the land to become river, lake, stream.

As one gazes upward and around, it seems as if the blue horizon touches down to the earth or water all around. At the same time, water comes from above in the form of rain. A simple explanation is that the sky, called the firmament, is solid, like an upside-down blue bowl covering the world. Rain is a great flood of water held up off the earth by the firmament. Rain falls when "windows" are opened in the firmament to let the water through. The sun, moon, stars are hung from the firmament like Christmas tree decorations.

This is the "scientific" view that prevailed when the Genesis story of creation came to life. By itself, it should be enough to warn us not to look for the answers to scientific puzzles in the Genesis story.

THE GENESIS STORY

"In the beginning, when God created the heavens and the earth."
The key word is "created," in Hebrew *bara'*. The content of this word comes from studying how the word is used in the Bible.

This study brings four insights into the word *bara'*:
1. It is used exclusively for divine activity. For anything that man might make or "create," other Hebrew words are employed.
2. It carries with it the notion of effortlessness, of sovereign activity. All is done with complete control and ease. God simply says, "Let there be . . .," and it happens. Notice how different this is from Enuma Elish where there is a conflict between divine powers, a war, a killing.
3. When the word is used, there is no mention of material from which God creates.
4. What God *"bara'-s"* is something new. Here in Genesis, God creates the cosmos which did not exist before. In Isaiah, the other Book where the word is most extensively used, God brings about a new order of salvation by his creative activity.

Simply from the use of this word, then, we understand that everything is made by God, and only by him; that his work of creation is very different from any human activity; that his work is the result of his tremendous power.

"The earth was a formless wasteland, and darkness covered the abyss, while a mighty wind swept over the water."
What a dismal picture! A nightmare! Darkness; a bleakness pervading; chaotic waters roaring; and over all, a howling hurricane. This is as close to the notion of nothingness that a person of those times could reach. This is the

picture of uncontrolled disorder, turbulence, chaos.

The important words are "formless wasteland." In his work of creation, God brings form to the formless and fills the wasteland with life.

On the first set of three days, God brings form to the formless by acts of division: light from darkness; the waters above the firmament from those below; water from land. On the second set of three days, God fills the wasteland by acts of embellishment for the area he has made by separating light from darkness — sun, moon, stars. For the water under the firmament, fish; and for the space opened by pushing the waters above the earth outside the firmament, birds. For the land, animals and people.

To put this into schematic form:

God Brings Form to the Formless: First Day, light/darkness, Genesis 1. 3-5; Second Day, lower/upper water, Genesis 1. 6-8; Third Day, water/land, Genesis 1. 9-13.

God Fills the Wasteland: Fourth Day, sun, moon, stars, Genesis 1. 14-19; Fifth Day, fish/birds, Genesis 1. 20-23; Sixth Day, animals/mankind, Genesis 1. 24-31.

This framework is a neat literary device rather than a scientific statement. All the work of creation is divided into two types of work. These, in turn, are subdivided into two sets of threes which correspond to each other.

All of this fits still another picture, that of the seven-day week with rest on the sabbath. We have seen in dealing with the Ten Commandments that most peoples of the time that makes up the background of the Old Testament celebrated some day of rest. The Israelites kept this custom and gave it religious meaning. It became especially significant as a sign precisely at the time when P was put

together, when the Israelites were in exile or shortly thereafter.

Remember how Catholics used to be known very easily by
not eating meat on Fridays? At parties, at restaurants, at
dinners in the homes of friends, the Catholic ate fish or
cheese on Friday — and everybody knew by this that he
was a Catholic. Passing up the meat was a public sign that
identified Catholics and created a bond of unity among
them.

During the Exile, when so many of the Israelites were surrounded by people of alien religions, the sabbath became
an important sign to identify the Israelite and give him a
sense of belonging.

In the creation story, the sabbath, the seventh day rest,
is a work of God. And the lesson is: As God did, so
should man do. The exiled Israelite should keep the sabbath to remain a faithful Israelite.

But there is more. In creation, God is like an orderly
workman. Unlike the unruly gods of Mesopotamia, who
create out of factions and killing, God creates with perfect
harmony and order.

Everything is as it should be. Chaos and disorder were
not part of the original scheme of things. They must have
come later.

"Let us make man in our image, after our likeness."

The creation of man is going to be God's work with an
intensity surpassing all that he has already done. The story
emphasizes this by the solemnity of the scene.

God is depicted as pondering over this part of creation in
a way that he did not do with the others. Up until now,

it has been, "God said, 'Let there be . . .' " Here, God
sets his mind more determinedly on what he is about. "Let
us make man . . ." Then God's creative activity is under-
lined by the threefold repetition of *bara'* in verse 27. The
signals are all there to indicate that what is happening here
is very important.

Notice the meaning of "man." The context shows that
this is not another example of male chauvinism in which
woman is ignored. "God created *man* in his image; in the
divine image he created *him; male and female* he created
them." Clearly, "man" is to be taken in the generic sense
of "humans." "Man" in the passage includes "male and
female" and corresponds to "them."

The generic word for "Mankind" is "Adam." This is going
to be important in reading through the next section of
Genesis where Adam, rather than being a proper name, is
to be understood as referring to "the man." Hopefully,
women's lib persons will bear with the style of this book
which uses "man" in the sense of mankind, to include
both men and women. Stopping to specify this all the
time, or substituting "person" for "man" or "woman"
gets unwieldy.

Why "Let *us* make man in *our* image? " Why the plural?
While there is no absolutely certain answer, this is not the
Three Persons of the Trinity deliberating among themselves.
We are still many years away from such advanced theology.

One possibility is that this is part of the religious trap-
pings of the time. The gods were thought to live in heaven,
surrounded by a court of heavenly retainers and servants.
Adapted to the Israelite belief in Yahweh, "let us" is the
one true God conferring with the members of this circle.

Another possibility comes from the word for God used
here, Elohim. In Hebrew, this word is a plural, even though
only Yahweh is indicated. The "us" and "our" could be

grammatical, agreeing with the plural subject of the activity. "God (plural-Elohim) said 'Let *us* (agreeing with Elohim) make men in *our* (agreeing with Elohim) image'."

Beyond the grammatical, in the use of the plural, there may be some reflection of the majesty of God whose life is so rich that it takes a plural to express him.

Man is created in the *image and likeness* of God. How is man to be like God?

The characteristic of God that comes through forcefully in this creation story is God's dominion over creation, his making and keeping order in all that is. Man is created to reflect that same character of God. Verses 28-30 show man's control over everything. He is to rule over all creation and to imitate God by keeping order and peace in what God has entrusted to him. Twice, in verses 26 and 28, this is explicitly stated. Man is to have dominion over all. But that dominion is not for selfish exploitation. It is to maintain the situation that God created when he "Looked at everything he had made, and he found it very good."

THE LESSONS OF THE CREATION ACCOUNT

1. The crucial point that must not be missed is that we are not dealing with information about science or history, but with insights into God and man. To put it bluntly, it is not to be expected that the authors of this story knew more about the scientific details of creation than we do. They knew a great deal less because of the primitive state of scientific knowledge of the time. However, and this is what is really important, *they did know a great deal about God.*

2. God created, not by struggle or because he had to, but by a free act of his own will. Man and the universe exist

not because there was no other possibility but because God willed them to. Whatever the details of the processes by which the universe and all that is in it came to be, all happens because God has so determined.

3. God has power over all creation. This is symbolized in the giving of the name to the works of creation. To give a name to someone or something means to put it into its proper place. For example, to be able to call this arrangement of wood "table" is to give it its category in the order of things. To be able to paint on a boat "Star" or "Sleepy Sue" or "Tonto III" is to demonstrate ownership. When it says that God names all the work of creation, the Bible is saying that the universe belongs to him.

4. Man is the high point of creation. He shares in God's rule of the created order. Man is God's representative to keep God's harmony and goodness in creation.

5. God is not a part of creation. He stands above and beyond and before all else that is. The visible world had a definite and absolute beginning. But God controlled that beginning and transcends it.

6. Though God is distinct from all of creation, he is deeply involved with it. He touches all that is. God is, at the same time, the One who transcends all else but whose hand and power and presence can be found in what he has made.

SUGGESTIONS FOR REFLECTION

1. Young persons spend much time during their adolescent years pondering the same questions as the Israelites: Who am I? Where do I come from? What is life all about? Have you wrestled with these questions? Have you ever tried to explain to anyone else your answers to them? Can you understand how stories or myths might have developed to explain them?

2. Since a myth is an attempt to explain the ultimate truth about man or life difficult to describe, try to recall a myth you learned as a child and the truth it was depicting.

3. Compare or contrast the Enuma Elish Epic and the Genesis story of creation.

4. Show how the Genesis narration of six days of creation followed by a sabbath of rest is not meant to be taken literally but is an intricate teaching device.

5. The creation account in the Bible is a highly theological statement telling much about the nature of God. Try to recall several points it makes about God. In what way was man seen to be in the image and likeness of God?

6. What new insights into the creation narrative have you received from reading this chapter? Do they have meaning for your own relationship with God?

CHAPTER VIII

THE LORD PLANTED A GARDEN IN EDEN

THE MAN, THE WOMAN, THE SERPENT, THE TREE

But what happened? If all that Genesis 1.1-2.4a affirms about the goodness of God and the world is true, where does the evil, confusion, and disorder that flood the world come from?

Reality and experience force you and me to ask this question. Old Testament man asked the same question long before we came along.

Please read: Genesis 2. 4b-3, 24

Notice how this section ends. God is portrayed as laying punishment on man and woman.

3.16 describes woman's situation — suffering in childbirth, a yearning for man which would bring its own grief since man would dominate her.

In 3.17-3.19, man comes in for his share of unhappiness. The reluctant soil will produce food necessary for sustenance only through man's drudgery. Man's lot will be to labor to keep himself alive until the time comes when death reduces his lifeless corpse to dust.

Sound familiar? It should. These verses, once adaptations are made for a change in culture, describe the human situation. People suffer in basic roles, in making a living. People suffer in their relationships with one another; husband to wife, parent to child. People suffer because the earth cannot be controlled by man. Drought and flood destroy plans. Wasteland and jungle fight being tamed to man's purposes. In more modern time, abuse of the earth has polluted rivers and air and endangered mankind's very survival.

In one chapter in Genesis, we have gone from "God looked at everything he had made, and he found it very good," to this woeful picture. Why? Why? Why?

The answer Genesis proposes is that if this deterioration has taken place, the fault is with man, not God. God created things good and meant them to remain that way. Man is the spoiler.

Again, we must affirm that these chapters are not modern history or science. Rather than literal description, what is portrayed here is a story of relationships that answers the question, "Where did evil come from? "

The central characters in these two chapters are "the man" and "the woman." The woman is not called "Eve" until after the harm is done in 3.26. The man is not called "Adam" as a proper name until 4.25 when the drama of Paradise is long over. This suggests again that we may be dealing with more than the personal history of two individuals. This is a portrayal of sin and relationships that remains true for all men always.

MAN IN THE GARDEN

The garden in Eden, Paradise, is not a place but a situation. The ideal situation intended by God is painted in vivid colors.

What are the imaginings that appeal to us? Advertisers know them. In the middle of the summer, TV screens fill with pictures of frosty glasses of beer or bottles of soft drink in a running stream. On muggy days when the temperature reaches 100, such little things seem like — Paradise!

When the wind howls around the windows, the cold bites deep, and the snow makes roads impassable, air line hucksters flash before us pictures of golden beaches, bathed in sun, washed with blue water, and ask us how we can afford not to head for that paradise.

For people in the often barren, dry and scorched lands of the Near East, the impossible dream was a plentiful supply of water, shady coolness, dewy trees, rich green shrubs and grass, food-plants that grew almost by themselves.

The garden in Eden is this dream. It is impossible to locate such a place as Eden. The names of the rivers are no real help. What is important about them is that the water flowing in Eden is so abundant that it divides into four great rivers to water a large part of the Near East. The garden of Eden is a symbol for an ideal situation.

There is more to this ideal situation. There is a "tree of life." This "tree of life" is common enough in the lands of the Bible. In Egypt, a great and ancient temple has a relief of the Pharaoh reaching out to pluck from a tree the *ankh,* the Egyptian symbol for eternal life. An ancient epic from Mesopotamia tells how its hero searched for eternal life and was given it in the form of a plant. But a serpent stole the plant from him.

The "tree of life" represents the truth that in the ideal situation intended by God, man was to be free from death, at least from death as a penalty, death as something to be feared.

Within the ideal situation was another possibility. This is symbolized in the "tree of the knowledge of good and bad." "To know" or "knowledge" in Hebrew is never simply an intellectual operation. It always involves the actual experience and possession of what is known. A common example is the phrase "to know a woman." "Knowing a woman" involves not simply recognizing or understanding a woman, but sexual intercourse.

As for "good and bad," other uses of this combination in the Old Testament suggest that "good and bad" equals "everything possible." Thus, "to know good and evil" is "the power to experience everything possible." "The tree" in the situation is a possibility that exists for man to make his own choices, to experience on his own terms whatever exists.

However, God tells man that he is not to pick and choose what to do and what not to do on his own terms. The man is told to trust God. God will keep him in the ideal situation if man will choose and decide according to the lines indicated by God. Of course, such a willingness to accept God's direction presumes an understanding that God loves and wishes only what is true and good for those to whom he gives directions.

THE WOMAN

Woman did not have an easy time in the cultural background against which this story is told.

Her life was difficult. The ordinary tasks of daily life were terribly wearing. To carry water from well to home; to grind grain for flour; to gather wood for the fire; to help in the fields; to tend the home and children. All these filled her day, and all were back-breaking toil.

Beyond this, woman generally had no rights of her own. A man, whether her husband or father, was her master. We have already seen in treating of the Ten Commandments that the command against adultery illustrates a general attitude. It was not a protection for woman as such but a safeguard for the rights of her husband. His wife belonged to him, and any other man who had sexual relations with her was violating the husband's rights. In the Near East, as far as can be determined, only the husband had the right to divorce. Generally wives and daughters had no right of inheritance. Such laws indicate the legal and social status of women.

If woman had any special place of honor, it was because of her sexual role. Only her body could give a man sons; sons who could work with him in his fields, or with his flocks; sons who would carry on his name and memory when he had passed on to the emptiness of death. Further, her body could provide man with intense pleasure. Because of this, even though her individual person was treated with little dignity, her sexual role was made divine. Statues of goddesses have been found with the sexual parts exaggerated. Even this divinizing of the sexual role did little to improve the living conditions of women.

With this as background, Genesis 2.20 mentions how man gave names to all the birds and animals, "but none proved to be the suitable partner for the man." Of all that God placed in creation, nothing was like man. Man was unique.

But when woman is created, man cries out in joy, "This one, at last, is bone of my bones and flesh of my flesh." The woman, of all the works of creation, is the only equal of man. Only she is the same kind of being that he is. To a culture which put down woman, which often degraded her, this story shouts "Not so! " Woman is like man. Woman is man's partner for life. Woman is made by God as the equal of man.

This equality is directed to a purpose. Man had been given responsibility for the created world. Now he has a help-mate, a partner in that responsibility. Man and woman together are to care for the earth which God has entrusted to them.

Once more, it is necessary to point out that the issue here is not a scientific discussion about how woman came to be. The rib is part of a story communicating a truth. The point at issue is teaching about relationships. God created man and woman equal and gave them responsibility for their earth.

That this teaching is to be found here does not necessarily mean that all its implications were understood and lived up to then any more than they are now.

THE SERPENT

Into the situation of God's good world, of peace, of man and woman and all creation in harmony, enters the villain.

Why a serpent? The answer must come from the culture of the time.

Snakes were often found near the springs and streams which could turn dead, dry land into living green fields. Snakes shed their skin, which seemed to be the sloughing off of an old body. Further, the serpent is an obvious phallic symbol. All of these factors connected the snake with life and fertility in the minds of the inhabitants of the Near East.

In Canaan, the land in which the Israelites eventually settled, the snake was a symbol of the god, Baal. The serpent conveyed the message that Baal was the god of fertility, of power, of restoration of life. Further, in the religious symbolism of Canaan, the serpent was a symbol of wisdom and shrewdness.

While the story of Eden was taking shape, Baal, the god of Canaan, was the great rival of Yahweh. Thus, in the original telling of the story, the hearers would have understood from the mention of a snake that an evil force, an evil power, was coming on the scene. From the terrible consequences of listening to the serpent, they would also have been warned off from any involvement with the pagan god represented by the snake.

This is not too different from our ability to pick out the bad guy in a straightforward, old-fashioned Western from the way he looks, even before he says or does anything.

This character, suspect by the very fact that he is portrayed as a serpent, challenges the way to life and wisdom that has been offered by God.

God has made continued life in the situation of peace and order and harmony dependent on trust in him. For man's life to be all that it should and could be, God asks for reliance on him.

The opposite is offered by the tempter. The serpent insinuates that the man and the woman should not trust God, that there is a mean selfishness in God which is imposing a shackling way of life on man. God does not really wish men to reach their full potential, to live out all the possible dimensions opening off life. The serpent entices the woman by telling her that if she eats of the fruit of the tree of good and bad, she and her man will become like gods.

In more abstract language, man and woman are tempted to make their own decisions about everything, to reject their status as creatures who stand before God, to spurn any relationship of trust in God because of the nagging suspicion that God may be holding something back. The temptation is to say, "I will do what I want to do, and by living this way, I will become more than just human. I will touch the fullness of life."

The woman listens to the temptation. She judges God and his way and finds it wanting. The man joins her.

THE AFTERMATH

Surely this should be the shining hour of man and woman!
They have stood side by side in affirming their own independence. They have acted as they chose. Hand in hand,
man and woman should now walk down the paths of history, united, fulfilled, happy.

But that is not what happens. In the story, the ideal situation crumbles in ruins.

God, whose intimacy with man is described in terms of his
walking in the garden, comes again. Only this time, the
man and the woman cannot face him. "The man and his
wife hid themselves from the Lord God among the trees of
the garden." The intimacy is gone. The honeymoon between God and the wonderful beings he has made to share
his life and power is over. Instead of being able to stand
tall and free and open before God, the pitiful creatures who
have asserted their independence, their maturity, their coming of age, must cringe out of sight of God.

One would expect that having shared their assertion of independence, being bound by a common rejection of God,
the man and woman would at least be drawn closer together.
But no! When God confronts the pair with their deed, the
man is willing to toss the woman to the dogs to save his
own neck. "The woman whom you put here with me —
she gave me fruit from the tree, and so I ate it." Every
man for himself! The same man who had so joyfully
shouted, "This is someone just like me," when first he met
the woman now points her out as the cause of his downfall.
The harmony and unity intended between the man and the
woman is a thing of the past.

Then come the rest of the disorders. The natural relationships between man and woman will continue to be distorted.

"Your urge shall be for your husband, and he shall be your master." The natural roles of man and woman will become a cause of pain. "In pain shall you bring forth your children."

Even nature will rebel against the dominion of man which God had intended. The harmony between man and nature will be ruined. "In toil shall you eat its (the ground's) yield all the days of your life. Thorns and thistles shall it bring forth to you, as you eat of the plants of the field. By the sweat of your face shall you get bread to eat."

At the end waits death. "Until you return to the ground from which you were taken; for you are dirt, and to dirt you shall return."

LIGHT IN THE DARKNESS

Even this picture of the failure of man to be what God intended him to be and of the drastic consequences of that failure is not without hope.

Genesis 3.14-15, God's decree of punishment for the serpent, contains a glimmer of hope for the future.

God says to the serpent, "I will put enmity between you and the woman, and between your offspring and hers; he will strike at your head, while you strike at his heel."

The history and interpretation of this passage are complex. Christian tradition has seen with the eyes of later faith into the message.

The original authors professed that God had reigned in the ideal situation through Adam/the man. Seeing with a broad vision of the future that does not specify times or details, the passage proclaims that God will once again reign by conquering the powers of evil. He will do this once again through a man.

In the light of what actually did occur, we know that the passage can be interpreted as fulfilled in Jesus. Through him, the head, the vital part of evil, will be crushed.

Another sign of hope appears in the seemingly insignificant statements in Genesis 3.20-21. "The man called his wife Eve, because she became the mother of all the living." Man, with almost heroic determination despite the disaster he has brought on himself, calls his wife, "the mother of the living." Despite sin and the pain and disorder unleashed, life will go on.

Genesis 3.21 says: "For the man and his wife the Lord God made leather garments with which he clothed them." Even here, there is a simple reason for hope. In 3.7, the man and woman had made loincloths for themselves out of leaves. Here, a compassionate God gives leather garments to clothe and protect the unfortunate creatures who have come from his hand. God's care will not cease but will touch man despite all that has happened.

UNANSWERED QUESTIONS

Many prominent issues have not been discussed. What about the problem of monogenism versus polygenism? Were there only one or many sets of first parents? How about evolution?

What would life have been like if there had been no sin?

What about the superhuman powers that tradition has attributed to the man before sin?

How talk about sin being transmitted from one generation to another, as we have to in the discussion of "original sin?"

There are two ways to consider original sin. One is to

try to look at original sin at its beginnings. What was the situation of the historically first sin? Who committed it? What was life like before that sin was committed?

The other view focuses on original sin as it exists today. The concern is with the effects and impact of sin on our lives here and now.

In this treatment, we have left aside trying to determine the original situation of man and woman, except to say that it was good. This is not to deny that further understanding may help us to see more deeply into a great many questions, or at least to speculate about such things. Nor is this a denial of the legitimacy of such investigation.

We have, however, preferred to stay with what is more certain in these verses. A very clear picture is sketched of the nature and meaning of sin. This is done through a story about man and woman.

This story teaches that evil is in the world because of the perverse choices of humans. God created men to trust in him to reach fulfillment and life. But he also created men free and able to make choices. Sin is the reality that occurs when man prefers to make his choices apart from God, when man decides to act as if he were the explanation and full meaning of his own existence, when man acts as if there were no one beyond himself.

When man behaves this way, he does not simply create an unpleasant situation between himself and God. This behavior is such a distortion of what was meant to be that he disrupts his relationships with all other humans. This is so because when a person does not understand his own dignity and status before God, he certainly will not recognize anyone else's. In such a situation, others become pawns to be moved about, puppets to be manipulated to serve one's own purposes. Or else others become obstacles to getting what one wants. And, of course, obstacles must be knocked down or climbed over or crushed.

If God is not the center of life, oneself inevitably will be.

What is true of relationships with others becomes true of relationships to the rest of creation. Once a person breaks down his real status before God, he will misuse the created world, and this will rebel against him, eventually stifling the possibilities of life.

Whatever Genesis says about Adam and Eve, it says a great deal about you and me.

This is an accurate picture of sin in our lives. It is a startlingly insightful picture of temptation, of the unwillingness to follow the way signaled by God. It is a portrayal in all its starkness of the crucial decision we all must face to accept or not accept that God has nothing else in mind for us except our own happiness, that the way of life he expects is not an arbitrary cramping of our style but the most authentic, real and human kind of life possible which opens up to life forever with God.

SUGGESTIONS FOR REFLECTION

1. Which do you regard as more harmful, more painful — a break in human relationships: e. g., between husband and wife, between parent and child, etc.; or nature run wild, e. g., droughts, floods, pollution, etc.? Do you ever connect these with sin? Do you think a break in relationship with God is actually more or less painful than either of these?

2. A popular theory of evolution today includes polygenism, which holds that at some moment in history, there was a "human being explosion," a number of simultaneous "first parents." Could this theory still be in accord with the narration of Genesis 1-3?

3. In the Genesis story, God gave Adam and Eve a powerful gift, freedom to choose. Although man's happiness will come only through choices that harmonize with God's direction for him, the opposite possibility is still open to him in his decision-making. As a parent or teacher, do you consider it a good educational tactic to have total respect for the freedom of the learner, even when he may make what seem to be poor choices? Where does trust enter the relationship? What has maturity to do with it?

4. "If God is not the center of life, oneself inevitably will be." How can you yourself grow, and help others to grow, more centered in God and less centered in self? Are any of us capable of doing this?

5. After reading this chapter, how would you define or describe "Sin?" Is this definition or description the one you grew up with? The one you hold today? What are its implications for religious education and young peoples' formation?

6. What new insights did you receive from this chapter regarding the following: the role of woman, paradise, the problem of evil, the meaning of work, the breakdown of relationships, original sin, who God is, and the meaning of good and evil?

CHAPTER IX

THE BEGINNING OF THE END

In Genesis 3-11, the story of sin continues. Once let loose
on the world, sin is like a huge avalanche roaring down a
mountain, catching up and sweeping away everything in
its path.

The story of Cain and Abel shows how evil becomes more
perverse. Whereas Adam and Eve stood against God by
refusing to trust in him, their son commits the horrible
crime of killing a brother. So distorted have relationships
become!

Eventually the world becomes so corrupt that the only way
to deal with it is to destroy it with the flood.

The Tower of Babel is another aspect of man's pride. Man
wishes to reach up to the heavens, to the very abode of God
himself until God puts an end to the scheming.

Each of these incidents needs more commentary on its details, historicity, background, and so forth, but the lesson is
consistent and emphatic.

Evil grows and corrupts all that it touches. Man's fate
seems hopeless. There appears to be no escape from sin.
Man can expect only to be tainted and destroyed by it.

But here the stories of Abraham begin. What man cannot
do by himself God does. The war between man and sin
is an unequal one if man must stand by himself. He cannot
put his trust in God. He cannot walk in God's ways.

God enters the battle on the side of the wonderful, yet pathetic, creature he has made.

Through history, God will show himself to be the kind of God he is in Genesis and Exodus, the God of creation and of liberation.

God's creation is not an act of the past, as if God had flung a universe into place and then let it go its own way. God had a purpose and plan in creation, a plan for good and peace and harmony. This has been disturbed by man's wilful use of his freedom. But God's creative power continues to act. God is constantly – God is now – creating the situation of peace and love he intended.

This situation will come about because God is also a liberator God. The primary Old Testament instance of that liberation was only a taste of the much greater liberation God intended – liberation from slavery to sin which could prevent man from ever reaching Life in its fullness. God's liberating activity also reaches here and now into our lives.

Since God works through men, Abraham is called to follow God's way, to do his part in the total plan of liberation and creation. Abraham, not seeing or understanding all, moves with God, becoming the model for all of us.

We are called now to follow God's way. For us, this way has been revealed in its fullness through Jesus Christ. Although we do not yet see the total picture intended by God, faith means we take our part in the loving creative and liberating activity of God by walking with his Son.

SUGGESTIONS FOR REFLECTION

1. Throughout the Books of Genesis and Exodus, we have seen God in his actions: lovingly creating, liberating, com-

passionately forgiving, providing for his creatures, respecting their freedom, ordering all things toward peace, harmony and reconciliation, etc. What other characteristics of God are revealed in these Books? In what ways do these Books especially call us to follow God's way?

2. Sometimes when we read the newspapers today, we feel the overwhelming corruption of sin. It is truly "like a huge avalanche roaring down a mountain, catching up and sweeping away everything in its path." The story of Abraham, describing how God "enters the battle on the side of the wonderful, yet pathetic, creature he has made," is a hope-filled message needed by our times. Can you point to any evidence that God is still acting in the world today, bringing it from despair, total corruption, and distortion, to re-creation and liberation? What would a newspaper front-page describing such activity look like?

3. Arrange these events in order of their occurrence in Israel's experience:
The composition of the book of Genesis
The Ten Commandments recorded
The Exodus from Egypt
The call of Abraham
The call of Moses
The plagues in Egypt

4. Thinking back over the chapters in this book, test your memory by trying to define or describe the following:
Covenant   Myth   Tree of Life   J E P traditions
The importance and meaning of "Name"   The "sin of Adam and Eve"   "Adam"   Etiology   "Apiru"
Angel of the Lord

SUGGESTIONS FOR FURTHER READING

Genesis 1-11
Genesis 12-50
Exodus
These are paperback booklets published as part of the *Old Testament Reading Guide* by the Liturgical Press, Collegeville, Minnesota.

The following are important, more advanced reference works containing commentaries on all the books of the Bible.

R. Brown, (ed.), *The Jerome Biblical Commentary.* Englewood Cliffs, N. J.: Prentice-Hall, 1968.

R. Fuller, (ed.), *A New Catholic Commentary on Holy Scripture.* London: Nelson, 1969.

C. Laymon, (ed.), *The Interpreter's One-Volume Commentary on the Bible.* Nashville: Abingdon Press, 1971.